CREATIVE LIFE

CREATIVE LIFE

CLARK E. MOUSTAKAS
The Merrill-Palmer Institute

D. VAN NOSTRAND COMPANY
New York   Cincinnati   Toronto   London   Melbourne

D. Van Nostrand Company Regional Offices:
New York   Cincinnati

D. Van Nostrand Company International Offices:
London   Toronto   Melbourne

Published by D. Van Nostrand Company
450 West 33rd Street, New York, N.Y. 10001

10   9   8   7   6   5   4   3   2   1

FOREWORD

For some time now I have been pursuing creative life, as it is lived by individual persons, as it enters into relationships, as it is reflected in nature and in universal ties. I have been exploring guiding principles that underlie creative life and the problems and challenges that threaten it and sometimes undermine it. I have been searching for a way to convey my perspectives and values regarding the powers of creative selfhood and the struggles to affirm it in the presence of social, school, and family pressures for conformity. The result is this series of essays presented in the language of vivid ideas, images, visions, and sensual acuities. The specific themes I focus on include individuality and encounter, dimensions of the creative life, the significance of honesty, sources of good and evil, and ethical and moral value. I am also interested in crises that precipitate periods of self-doubt and move the person to new awareness, resolution, and active changes in the self. I have included essays expressing my concerns regarding anger, its healthy and neurotic components, and the importance of silence, self-dialogue, and meditation in creative discovery.

I am ready to pause now and let *Creative Life* speak for itself. I am hopeful that it will evoke new awarenesses, that it will affirm the uniqueness of persons and support their struggles to be and to create, and that it will encourage a deepening value basis for life with others, life that is rooted in authenticity and honesty as well as in love. My purpose is to enhance and affirm, to awaken a new flow of life that will enable people to listen to themselves, to hear their own internal messages, and to connect fundamentally with other persons.

I want to thank all the people who helped me in this search, particularly my friend and colleague Cereta Perry; my graduate students at The Merrill-Palmer Institute; members of my workshops in Massachusetts, Maine, and California; the children and teachers from inner-city Detroit and suburban schools; and the authors and publishers listed at the end of each essay. I also express my appreciation to Michael Usdan, president of The Merrill-Palmer Institute, for his continued support and affirmation of humanistic approaches to research and writing. Finally, I thank Mavis Wolfe for her devotion and diligent help in typing the manuscript.

Clark E. Moustakas

CONTENTS

CREATIVE LIFE

CHAPTER 1

UNIQUENESS AND INDIVIDUALITY

PERHAPS THERE IS no tangible way to express the essence of what it means to be an individual, to be your own self and to connect fundamentally with other human beings. Sometimes in a spontaneous, exuberant rush of feelings, the words form, and the body comes alive. But in that instant I catch a glimpse of others and stop—it is a moment frozen by the presence of neutral and lifeless people. Whatever comes then has lost its power of movement and impact. Right in the middle of a flowing breath—the question, the frown, the disapproving glance; or just the indifferent or neutral face. I know I am not meeting the expectations of others; I am not following a typical path. But I stand on my own ground, and however difficult, I listen to the sounds within to discover what it means to stay alive as an individual.

Within every person is a distinct and unique being that is unlike any life that has existed before or will ever exist again. To maintain this uniqueness, when social and family pressures aim at suppressing or destroying it, is the ultimate challenge of every human being. The unique person remains distinctive by exploring, discovering, continually unfolding in new ways, and finding a sense of fulfillment in being rooted in life and creating new life. Boundaries that would restrict creation of life must be transcended and the restraints of conditioning overcome. Nietzsche, in *The Will To Power*, emphasizes the distinctive nature of individuality:

> The individual is something quite new which creates new things, something absolute; all his acts are entirely his own.
>
> Ultimately, the individual derives the values of his acts from himself; because he has to interpret in a quite individual way even the words he has inherited. His interpretation of a formula at least is personal, even if he does not create a formula: as an interpreter he is still creative (1).

1

The unique person encounters life with all available resources and lives in accordance with the particular requirements of each situation as it unfolds. Neither bounded by the past, nor fixed to the limits of the present, the creative person realizes new facets of individuality by continuing to respond to life in unique ways. A. H. Maslow has emphasized that when life is being created through the freedom and choice of the person, through the uniqueness of the individual, the human tendency is to go on to more complex, richer experiences and accomplishments (2). The person experiences a feedback effect in feelings of capability, mastery, self-trust, and self-esteem.

The realization of one's uniqueness is felt during silences and self-reflections, in times of loneliness and solitude, and in moments of communion with others. Thus, it is essential that each person be aware that genuine life is created through unique potentials, resources, and preferences, and that this truth is reaffirmed when the individual pauses to recognize, support, and encourage his or her own personal tendencies.

Kierkegaard wrote in one of his journals: "There is a view of life which conceives that where the crowd is, there also is the truth, and that in truth itself there is need of having the crowd on its side . . . a crowd in its very concept is the untruth, by reason of the fact that it renders the individual completely impenitent and irresponsible, or at least weakens his sense of responsibility by reducing it to a fraction. . . . No, when it is a question of a single individual man, then is the time to give expression to the truth by showing one's respect for what it is to be a man" (3).

The experience of any person is real only when it is being lived; when it is talked about or explained something essential is lost. Efforts to define the real self inevitably distort its reality and violate the integral nature of life. To define the self we must categorize and compare and treat the person as a list of traits. The real self is not known through diagnosis, analysis, and evaluation; these methods destroy its unity and leave only bits and pieces.

The self exists as a whole, with enduring presence and emerging patterns. Because of its uniqueness, depth, and changing nature its qualities or states may be felt as reflections of an inconceivable totality or whole. The self of the individual may stand out in bold relief, or it may blend imperceptibly with other forms in nature and in the universe. It may be recognized through intuitive and unusual sense perceptions.

When the person is free to explore capacities and discover

meanings and values, an essential step is being taken in the creation of an identity. Other persons facilitate this process by their willingness to enter the unique world of the individual, and by their clear and direct acceptance. In this way the individual is supported and encouraged to move forward. Choosing in accord with one's nature is the way to growth, the way to retain the subjective experiences of delight or boredom as the *criteria* of correct choice (4). The alternative is making the choice in terms of other's wishes. When this happens the individual is restricted to safety needs alone, giving up the delight criterion out of fear of loss of protection and love. We assist a person to be present as a unique self by our own willingness to steep ourselves temporarily in that person's world. By our affirmation, we support the next step in growth.

As long as a person maintains the integrity and uniqueness of individual nature, growth of the self (which begins at birth) continues throughout life. The urge to express one's individual nature and come to full self-realization lies within each person. It is neither a quiescent drive that must be activated by external pressures and motivations nor an effort to relieve tensions. On the contrary, the urge to *become* who one is meant to be is a positive force.

Only the individual can actualize the potentials of the self. By its nature the self is inclined to grow and move toward an evolving identity, an individuality that also has an irrevocable biological basis. Although tissues continually change, individual specificity persists during the entire life; although organs of the body move toward definitive transformations and death, they always maintain their unique qualities (5). Inherent in every higher organism is something that differentiates one individual from every other individual, a difference that can be seen by observing the reactions of certain cells and tissues belonging to one individual in contrast to the tissues and cells of another individual of the same species (6). To the extent that the intrinsic nature of the individual is nourished and cultivated, the person maintains the integrity of the self and moves toward originality of expression and actualization of potentials.

When a person is perceived primarily in terms of *whatness* (for example, age, size, sex, or class) rather than *whoness*, the vital core of the person is completely missed. When products are the basis for judgment and prediction, the becoming nature of the individual is totally ignored. Potential and promise are more clearly disclosed in the desire for life and the thirst for knowledge than in acquiring good marks or obtaining college degrees.

In spite of all the advances in personality tests, understanding the person from his or her own point of view, in the light of unique experiences, desires, and interests, is still the most real way of knowing that person. To really know another person one must come into real contact with the person's dreams and yearnings, fears and hopes, optimism and disillusion; one must understand the individual's own perceptions, preferences, and values. Most people are able to state their experiences honestly so that, in most instances, a straight question will get a straight answer.

The absurdity of relying on mechanical tests and devices rather than individuals themselves was revealed in a series of motivation studies. In these studies the projective tests failed to show the craving for food among men on a starvation diet (7). The number of food associations actually declined with longer periods of fasting. No one would question the importance of extreme hunger in motivating behavior, yet this motive was not uncovered by mechanical devices. It was, however, easily disclosed in conversations with the men. Self-statements, autobiographical accounts of interest, involvement, and motivation are potent and valid "facts" in understanding individuals and in making decisions regarding their readiness for new functions and activities, for positions, and for admission to schools and college programs.

We can understand the meaning that experiences have for others by listening to them with objectivity and attempting to understand the essence of the experience through the person's relating of it. Objectivity here refers to seeing what an experience *is* for another person, not how it fits in with or relates to other experiences—not what causes it, why it exists, or what purpose it serves. Being objective means seeing and understanding the feelings, concepts, beliefs, and values of an individual as they are at the moment the person expresses them. The experience of the other person as perceived is sufficient unto itself and can be understood in terms of itself alone.

Knowing only the content of an experience does not convey its unique meaning any more than knowing that a tree has a trunk and branches tells how it will be perceived by the different people who see it. The "facts" regarding human behavior have little meaning in themselves. It is the manner in which they are perceived and known that reveals how they will be expressed in behavior. Experiments at the Hanover Institute in Hanover, New

Hampshire, have shown that we do not receive our perceptions from the things around us, but rather that our perceptions come from within us (8). The premise underlying these studies was that the traditional mode of science—its objectives and methods of investigation—did not satisfy the requirements of human experience and the knowledge that comes from the experiencing individual (9). A science for the study of persons must consider the meanings that people derive from their experiences, and these meanings are based on actual thoughts, feelings, and perceptions. One of the demonstrations at the Hanover Institute showed that when an observer sees two star-shaped points of light at equal distances, the brighter point looks nearer. Or, when observing two lines of light at the same distance and elevation, the longer line looks nearer. On the basis of this and other perception experiments of Adelbert Ames, Jr., it was concluded that perception is a function of the perceiver, based on past experience and current prediction as guides to action (10, 11). It is clear that the individual is all-important in the process of perception.

Complex and thorough examination sometimes is required to diagnose tuberculosis, cancer, or a heart ailment; but knowing about the presence of a serious illness does not tell what it will mean to the sick person. A group of physicians may find it easy to communicate with each other regarding the nature of an illness but difficult to talk to the "patient" when they have not taken into account the "patient's" perceptions of the illness. When physicians question the impact of the patient's self-perceptions, they minimize the potential curative powers within the person and the strivings for health. This weakens the patient's self-confidence and reduces resources for recovery. To the extent that physicians fail to consider the patient's private experience, they do not understand the full nature of the illness. If they show complete confidence in medical aspects but little recognition of the patient as unique and special, they miss a critical dimension of the illness—the fact that in important ways each person is unlike any other who has had a painful disease.

When experts fail to recognize that facts attain meaning in a personal context and that the meaning differs for each person, they fail to understand fully the true nature of a fact. Generalizations about human growth and development do not apply to the particular person, and recommendations based on "facts," without reference to personal experience, are of questionable value. Rather than leading to constructive action, such recommendations frighten and immobilize the person and delay solution of the problem. This is certainly as true today as it was in Dickens' time, when the Thomas Gradgrinds of life were at all times regulated and governed by facts (12). Such people grew up like machines and were seriously disabled in their ability to settle issues in a healthy way.

When individuals are analyzed in terms of their fathers, mothers, siblings, or anyone else, their real nature is distorted. One cannot know another person by projecting onto that person someone else or by abstracting out of the person transferred feelings and attitudes. This approach conveys a fundamental disregard for and destructive attitude toward the person. The analytic attitude has a keen eye for the weaknesses of people but fails to recognize the core and essential nature of the individual, fails to recognize the internal life and personal meanings that significantly influence behavior (13).

All psychological phenomena can be understood as illustrating the single principle of unity or self-consistency (14). When the individual becomes a real person there is not only integrity and unity in experience but also fullness and variety. Harmony in life comes from an increasing capacity to find in the world what will register within the depths of one's own being (15).

Resistance to external pressure permits a person to maintain self-consistency. It is a healthy response, indicating that the will of the individual is still intact. It is the person's effort to sustain integrity. According to Assagioli, the function of the will is similar to that performed by the helmsman of a ship (16). The challenge is to know what one's path should be and to keep steadily on course, despite the drifts caused by wind and current. Concentration, mastery, persistence, determination, and initiative are all qualities of the will that are expressed when the person is self-directive. Within each person is a core of being, a last stronghold, so to speak, that resists attempts to push the person away from the self, to change the individual to meet others' expectations and demands. When we force a person to behave according to our own values, when we impose our convictions on the other person, we stifle creativity and the will to explore and actualize.

Otto Rank stressed the importance of will expression. He believed that individuality is essentially a matter of conscious willing and that neurosis is the consequence of failing to develop as an individual. He concluded that "the neurotic character represents not illness but a developmental phase of the individuality problem, a personality denying its own will, not accepting itself as an individual" (17).

Confronted by external pressures (attempts to frighten and force the person to submit to symbols, standards, and values from outside), a person must often call upon sources of life within, follow internal cues, and be intentionally assertive in order to retain an identity. If the person conforms while the core of being is in opposition, health and stability are jeopardized and the individual is unable to think, decide, or act. The imposition of expectations and values may force a person to wear masks of convention and propriety.

Expressions of the real self reflect the natural emergence of potentiality. They are unified and consistent in behavior, not the wild, confused, and fragmentary "acting out" often designated as self-expression. This kind of self-expression is a reaction to frustration, denial, and rejection, to not being a self. An authentic expression of the self must recognize personal individuality and also recognize the rights of others. As Reinhold Niebuhr has stated, "There is no point at which the self, seeking its own, can feel itself self-satisfied and free to consider others than itself. The concern for others is as immediate as the concern for itself" (18). Respect for one's own integrity and uniqueness, love for and understanding of one's own self are inseparable from the respect, love, and understanding of other persons (19). The creative expression of the self is often misunderstood. Rollo May has stated: "Those of us who lived in the 1920's can recall the evidences of the growing tendency to think of the self in superficial and oversimplified terms. In those days "self-expression" was supposed to be simply doing whatever popped into one's head, as though the self were synonymous with any random impulse, and as though one's decision were to be made on the basis of a whim which might be a product of digestion from a hurried lunch just as often as one's philosophy of life" (20).

If real expression of the self is a bad thing, the blame lies not with the self but with providence (21). Unless people are free to express their own uniqueness and distinctiveness, the capacity for growth is stifled and denied. Self-expression is the individual's way of asserting a definite *yes* or *no* response to life.

Wishes and desires are also important aspects of individuality and accentuate the particular ways of the person. Desire is not a blind and capricious impulse but a necessary urge that makes vital experience possible. It is actively surging forward to break through whatever dams it up. To desire is to want, to feel, to be free to choose. The person must know what he or she wants, though not necessarily in a conscious, deliberate way. Knowing what one wants is simply the elemental ability to choose one's own values.

As long as a situation has genuine appeal for a person, it is not necessary to ask what it is good for. As John Dewey has indicated, "This is a question which can be asked only about instrumental values. Some goods are not good *for* anything; they are just goods. Any other notion leads to an absurdity" (22).

When we reject the desires and interests of another person, we are also rejecting the person. Because the self exists as a whole, rejection of significant dimensions of the self is experienced by a person as rejection of the entire self. The expression, "I love you but not what you do," implies that a person exists in parts. Even if a person feels loving while rejecting the actions of another individual, the rejected person is split, with a part being confirmed and a part being condemned.

Rejection of another person through a rejection of behavior is tempered when we understand and appreciate the feelings or wishes of the other person involved. If we usually accept and value the person, the bonds established in the positive moments will sustain us in the rejecting moments. It takes courage to recognize and admit rejecting feelings for those whom we ordinarily cherish, but when the rejection is occasional, the feeling of love will endure in the relationship. The struggle between persons is always away from fragmentation of the self and toward an integration of persons as whole beings. Thus temporary rejection implies upheaval and conflict; the persons involved in the conflict, although basically accepting each other, seek a new pattern of relationship and a new level of unity.

Rejection often occurs because we fear that if we permit individuals to explore desires and interests in their own way they will develop antisocial tendencies or become lazy and indifferent. We feel we have to condition them, teach them directly, keep after them to socialize them and make them become "responsible" persons. When this happens, it is clear that we do not trust ourselves or have confidence that our own personal experiences with the other person will provide a healthy basis for social growth.

Somehow we must remove the beliefs that make people mistrust themselves and each other. Having the freedom to grow and to actualize one's self provides the best foundation for interacting with others within groups, and in society. One cannot grow according to one's own nature unless one is free—and to be free is to accept oneself in totality, to respect one's individuality, and to be open and ready to engage in new experience. Freedom also means selecting those human values that will foster growth. John Dewey states that freedom contains three important elements: (1) efficiency in action and the absence of cramping and thwarting obstacles, (2) capacity to change the course of action and to experience novelties, and (3) the power of desire and choice to be factors in events (23). Freedom includes a basic attitude of allowing one's self to be the guiding force in significant experience, allowing one's self to discover truth and to express it.

There can be no freedom without responsibility, but self-discipline and self-responsibility are inherent tendencies in people. To be positively free is to be simultaneously spontaneous and thoughtful, self-enhancing and other-enhancing, self-valuing and valuing of others. When people are free to be themselves in a way that includes self and other, trust is not violated. When individual integrity is maintained and fostered, society is enriched.

We must not accept as intrinsic the antagonism between individual interests and social interests. Maslow has strongly emphasized that this kind of antagonism exists only in a sick society (24). Individual and social interests are synergetic, not antagonistic. Thus, creative individual expression results in social creativity and growth—which in turn encourage and free the individual to further self-expression and discovery. What is true and of value to society emerges from genuine self-interest.

All people need love, safety, belongingness, acceptance, and respect as conditions basic to their growth. When these conditions are provided by the human environment, growth occurs naturally through actualization of one's potentials. We may offer resources, make available opportunities, and give information and help when it is needed. But to force standards, social values, and concepts on another person is to stifle potential creativity and difference. Relations must be such that individuals are free to affirm, express, actualize, and experience their uniqueness. We make this possible when we show that we deeply care for other persons, respect their individuality, and accept them without qualifications. To permit another person to be and become does not promote selfishness. Rather it affirms the self of the person and facilitates growth.

The following principles summarize a basic approach to the recognition of uniqueness and individuality:

1. The individual knows herself or himself better than anyone else.

2. Only the individual can develop the potentials of the self.

3. The individual's perceptions of reality are more valid than any outside diagnosis.

4. The individual, to keep on growing as a self, must continue to believe in herself or himself, regardless of what anyone else may think or prefer. The belief in one's own reality is a necessary condition to the fulfillment of that reality.

5. Objects have no meaning in themselves. Individuals give meanings to them. These meanings reflect the individual's background of experience.

6. Every individual is consistent and logical in the context of his or her own personal experience. The individual may *seem* inconsistent and illogical to others, however, when not understood and valued.

7. As long as individuals accept and value themselves they will continue to grow and develop their potentials. When they do not accept and value themselves, energies will be used to defend themselves rather than to explore and to actualize.

8. Every individual wants to grow toward self-fulfillment. These growth strivings are present at all times.

9. An individual learns significantly only those things that are involved in the maintenance or enhancement of self. No one can force the individual to learn. The person will learn only if he or she wills to. Any other type of learning is temporary and inconsistent with the self and will disappear as soon as the threat is removed (25, 26).

10. We cannot teach another person directly. We can make real learning possible by providing information and the appropriate setting, atmosphere, materials, and resources and by being there. The learning process itself is a unique, individual experience.

11. Under threat, the self is less open to spontaneous expression—that is, more passive and controlled. When free from threat, the self is open—that is, free to be and to strive toward actualization (25, 26).

12. The situation that most effectively promotes significant

learning is one in which (a) the threat to the self is at a minimum while at the same time the uniqueness of the individual is valued and respected; and (b) the person is free to make choices and to explore the materials and resources available in the light of personal interests, desires, and potentials.

To stay alive as an individual it is essential to keep in touch with oneself and to be aware of inner feelings, ideas, and shifts in perception. It is necessary to recognize, sense, and know one's response to life and, in spite of the forces that would diminish and reduce one's sense of self, to stand uniquely present—not becoming detached, shrewd, calculating, narrowly objective, but remaining open, continuing to feel, explore, and discover one's self as a spontaneous, receptive being (27). The challenge of knowing one's self is always present. There is always a choice between wearing a mask or being authentic and facing the reality of conflict and genuine encounter. In its varied forms, individuality is the good each person seeks in days of darkness and in days of light. Individuality emerges from deep levels of the self, from resources and talents that are within each of us to be formed and shaped through encounters with nature, others, and the world. The individual grows as a unique self when the senses are alive and active, when feelings are expressed openly and honestly, when being is valued for itself, when life is created freely from the individual's own convictions, values, and preferences.

REFERENCES

1. Nietzsche, Friedrich. *The Will To Power*. Ed. by W. Kaufmann. New York: Vintage, 1968, p. 403.

2. Maslow, A. H. *The Farther Reaches of Human Nature*. New York: Viking Press, 1971.

3. Kierkegaard, Soren. *A Kierkegaard Anthology*. Ed. by Robert Bretall. Princeton, N.J.: Princeton University Press, 1946.

4. Maslow, A. H. *The Farther Reaches of Human Nature*. New York: Viking Press, 1971.

5. Carrel, Alexes. *Man The Unknown*. New York: Harper Bros., 1935, p. 267.

6. Loeb, Leo. *The Biological Basis of Individuality*. Springfield, Ill.: Charles C. Thomas, 1945, p. 4.

7. Allport, Gordon W. "The Trend in Motivational Theory," *American Journal of Orthopsychiatry* 23 (1953): 107–119.

8. Kelley, Earl C. *Education for What Is Real*. New York: Harper Bros., 1947.

9. Cantril, Hadley; Ames, Jr., Adelbert; Hestorf, Albert H.; and Ittelson, William H. "Psychology and Scientific Research, I, The Nature of Scientific Inquiry." *Science* 110 (1949): 461–464.

10. Cantril, Hadley, ed. *The Morning Notes of Adelbert Ames*. New Brunswick: Rutgers University Press, 1960.

11. Ittelson, W. H., and Kilpatrick, F. P. "Experiments in Perception." *Scientific American* 185 (1951): 50–55.

12. Dickens, Charles. *Hard Times*. Greenwich, Conn.: Fawcett Publications, 1966.

13. Angyal, Andras. "A Theoretical Model for Personality Studies." *Journal of Personality* 20 (1951): 131–141.

14. Lecky, Prescott. *Self-Consistency: A Theory of Personality*. Ed. by Frederick C. Thorne. New York: Island Press, 1951.

15. Mooney, Ross. "Creation, Parents, and Children." *Progressive Education* 31 (1953): 14–17.

16. Assagioli, Roberto. *The Act of Will*. New York: Viking Press, 1973, p. 19.

17. Rank, Otto. *Will Therapy*. New York: Alfred A. Knopf, 1936, p. 49.

18. Niebuhr, Reinhold. *The Self and the Dramas of History*. New York: Charles Scribner's Sons, 1955, p. 139.

19. Fromm, Erich. *Man for Himself: An Inquiry into the Psychology of Ethics*. New York: Rinehart & Co., 1947.

20. May, Rollo. *Man's Search for Himself*. New York: W. W. Norton & Co., 1953, p. 56.

21. Dewey, John. *Human Nature and Conduct*. New York: Henry Holt & Co., 1922, pp. 1–13.

22. Dewey, John. *Democracy and Education*. New York: Macmillan Co., 1916, p. 283.

23. Dewey, John. *Human Nature and Conduct*. New York: Henry Holt & Co., 1922, pp. 303–304.

24. Maslow, A. H. "The Instinctoid Nature of Basic Needs." *Journal of Personality* 22 (1954): 326–347.

25. Rogers, Carl R. *Client-Centered Therapy*. Boston: Houghton Mifflin Co., 1951.

26. Rogers, Carl R. *On Becoming A Person*. Boston: Houghton Mifflin Co., 1961.

27. Moustakas, Clark. *Individuality and Encounter*. Cambridge, Mass.: Howard Doyle Publishing Co., 1968.

CHAPTER 2

THE SENSE
OF SELF

R EMAINING IN TOUCH with one's own self is the
first requirement for continuing personal growth.
No matter how different my experience is from
that of others, to evolve as a unique being I must trust in the
validity of my own senses. To the extent that I respect the
authenticity of my own experience, I will be open to new levels of
learning, to new pathways of relatedness, and to a genuine respect
for all of life. When I am guided by the real nature of my
experience, I am ready to share resources and talents and ready to
enter into full communion with other persons.

Genuine relating is a process of intuitive awareness, sensing,
and knowing—not an intellectual, objective, detached thought
process that judges and classifies others. Genuine relating involves a recognition of the mystery and awe, the capriciousness
and unpredictability of life. It means trusting unknown develop-
ments in experience and willingness to follow the uncertain
course that results in a creative realization of one's own
potentialities.

My own approach to human relations has been a growing
awareness of the significance of mystery and uncertainty, an
awareness of the value of suffering and grief as well as of joy and
happiness, and an awareness of the power of silence and of real
dialogue in the deep moments of life within myself and with
others.

Once, as I sat with a person, I concentrated on that person's
every word and motion, deliberately trying to comprehend exact
meanings. Using my resources to understand, to see through and
beyond fumbling ways and distortions of reality, I searched for
basic intentions and feelings. I tried to help the individual release
inner tensions, achieve a sense of inner harmony, and restore integrity. I attempted to understand, to clarify, to say just the right
words that would bring the other person to a higher level of
comfort or comprehension. If only I could help that person see

13

how in renouncing wishes and interests and ways a unique heritage and destiny were being denied. If only I could help the
person realize that she or he was a worthy self and that even
though everything else were lost, the potential for new life
remained, and that potential could never be taken away. To
realize, to understand, to see with greater clarity, deeper meaning,
and insight, to bring the pieces together into a comprehensible
whole—on these depended my success or failure.

But what was being clarified? What was being understood?
And what did the uncovering of missing links and relinking the
whole provide? What did examination of a relationship render?
Only a self in pursuit of understanding others? Only a series of
reactions and interchanges and influences? Only an unbroken
chain of associations and events? Only an organization of discrete
items? Only a clarification of what the other person says and does,
of habits and attitudes, of projection and defenses? Is this a life being lived fully in the human sense? Is this a self growing as a self,
in touch with inner resources and in correspondence with nature
and other selves?

There is no doubt that the unique human gifts of logic and
reasoning are of great value in clarifying ideas, understanding
basic causes and motivations, solving problems, uncovering hidden meanings, meeting challenges, and making decisions. But
reasoning and logic are only pieces of man engaged in certain
kinds of intercourse with the universe. There are also the
experiences of pain and suffering; of love and beauty; of the sun,
the stars, the mountains, and the seas. There is faith in God, and
the food I share with my brother or sister, and the walk I take on a
silent moonlit night, and the games I play with my children.
There is loneliness and a sense of being apart—even when part of
a group life. Are there not many, many human experiences of fantasy and wonder and imagination, beyond logic and beyond
reason, in which it takes courage to live with oneself or to share
with others, long before there is any understanding or insight or
clarification, long before there is any separated knowledge or
comprehension?

In Dickens' *Hard Times* the deadening consequences of hard
facts is dramatically portrayed in Thomas Gradgrind's relationship with his children. There were five Gradgrinds and every one
of them a model child; "lectured at from their tenderest years;
coursed, like little hares." In a powerful scene, one child, Louisa,
speaks of the tragic affect of this systematic denial of her senses:

"Yet, father, if I had been stone blind; if I had groped my way by my sense of touch, and had been free, while I knew the shapes and surfaces of things, to exercise my fancy somewhat, in regard to them, I should have been a million times wiser, happier, more loving, more contented, more innocent and human in all good respects, than I am with the eyes I have" (1).

Louisa's father never knew her, for the dead facts did not disclose her as a living person in the heights and depths of being, in the ups and downs of darkness and sunlight, in the ranges of feelings, and in the living spirit that comes in its own time in silence and in real words. The freedom to sense and feel with fancy, with imagination, with drama, and with mystery is essential in every awakening of the self. There are many situations in which I am totally involved in the mystery of being who I am—isolated hours of quiet self-reflection, lonely self experiences, moments with a congenial friend. There are times when I feel related to a falling leaf, to an isolated flower on a frosty day, to thunder and wind and rain, when all is related to all and belongs to all and remains as it is, when ecstasy and fantasy merge into new dreams and new life. William Wordsworth conveys such a sense of self in this poem:

> I have felt
> A presence that disturbs me with the joy
> Of elevated thought; a sense sublime
> Of something far more deeply interfused,
> Whose dwelling is the light of setting suns,
> And the round ocean and the living air,
> And the blue sky, and in the mind of man—
> A motion and a spirit, that impels
> All thinking things, all objects of all thought,
> And rolls through all things (2).

Are experiences like these not important in the creation of the self? Yet where is the understanding and the comprehension? What concept or definition, what thoughtful essay could ever communicate the wonder and awe of holistic experience when a person is real, and a tree is a tree, and the dawn is the dawn, yet each merges into the other, and each gives meaning to the other, and in unity they create something entirely new—a poetry of living form.

Maslow has emphasized that in peak experiences it is characteristic that the universe is perceived as an integrated and unified whole: "To have a clear perception (rather than a purely abstract and verbal philosophical acceptance) that the universe is all of a piece and that one has his place in it—one is a part of it, one belongs in it—can be so profound and shaking an experience that it can change the person's character and his Weltanschauung forever after" (3). In his book *Cosmic Consciousness*, Richard Bucke reports such a transformation in the creation of the self in the experience of a woman who had suffered deeply before a sudden, strange submission and awakening.

> "I had learned the grand lesson, that suffering is the price which must be paid for all that is worth having; that in some mysterious way we are refined and sensitized, doubtless largely by it, so that we are made susceptible to nature's higher and finer influences—this, if true of one, is true of all. And feeling and knowing this, I do not now rave as once I did, but am silent as I sit and look out upon all the sorrow of the world. . . .
>
> My feeling is as if I were as distinct and separate from all other beings and things as is the moon in space and at the same time indissolubly one with all nature" (4).

Many revelations of the self are a mystery. One can participate in them, share them, live them in the existential sense. But it is absurd to try to understand what is inexplicable; to derive motivation, purpose, and goal from what is simple and clear. What is a mystery is a mystery—life is a mystery, and death, and creations of the self and of the universe. It is this mystery, this unknown ecstasy of life, that in present-day society is not embraced and valued, but too often ignored, neglected—or merely analyzed and understood. Albert Guerard speaks of this universal mysticism in his book *Bottle in the Sea*.

> . . . Whether you think in terms of a grace parsimoniously imparted from above, or of a seed growing through the whole of mankind, the mystic experience, in its full directness and intensity, is rare in our days, and it is uncertain. Not only are ordinary mortals skeptical about such a transcendental gift, but the favored ones themselves have their hours of doubt and despair. . . . The ineffable imposes

silence. It cannot be comprehended, it cannot be remembered, it leaves no intelligible trace. There remains with us only an undefinable longing for a truth, for a peace, for a love passing all understanding (5).

This dimension—call it spiritual or mystic or aesthetic, or creative, or simply human beings being human at an ultimate, or peak, level—that I am speaking about refers to unknown forces in the individual merging with unknown forces in the universe and letting happen what will, permitting reality to grow in its fullest sense and letting the unpredictable in oneself encounter the unpredictable in the other. Then a breakthrough of self occurs in which the individual does the unexpected and is newly born, perceiving, sensing, and experiencing in a totally different way. The process is facilitated through patience. Again and again in my work with others patience is singled out as a key in the emergence of mystery, opening, awareness, struggle, new experience. Active, committed waiting often precedes other catalysts in the growth process. Active waiting with oneself and with others is a form of belief and trust in the powers of the self; a belief that something of value exists long before there is direct evidence or support for it. This trust in the unknown and patience in waiting for a new beginning is too often denied.

How can individuals develop latent resources and hidden talents when they are constantly being urged to conform, to compete, to achieve, to evaluate, to establish fixed goals? How can the uniqueness of the person take form in a living situation when the person is continually being pressured to communicate in precise ways and to become a model along the usual norms and standards?

We live in an age of reasoning in which the self is a self-system, a series of rationalities and concepts, in which skills are used to exploit and manipulate, in which abstractions are more relevant than the realities abstracted, and in which the symbol has become more real than the person or thing symbolized. Ours is an age of comfort, ready to receive and consume, in which it is easier to stay within the known and safe limits of life than it is to plunge into new relations and experiences; in which it is safer to accept the usual and regular facts in the usual and regular ways; in which it is better to keep quiet and look away whenever there is a vibrant cry for justice and truth; in which it is better to remain on the edges of a real relationship because a genuine meeting might bring pain, suffering, and grief. We live in a time of machines and technological advances and techniques and procedures, when one can get a list of approved ways to observe and act for almost any situation. In *The Zen of Seeing* Frederick Franck boldly states, "We do a lot of looking; we look through lenses, telescopes, television tubes. . . . Our looking is perfected every day—but we see less and less. . . . Ever more gadgets, from cameras to computers, from art books to videotapes, conspire to take over our thinking, our feeling, our experiencing, our seeing" (6).

We live in an age of adjustment, when the individual is forced into group modes and preferences—either by authority or popular vote. Unanimity, however, is neither practical nor expedient, because individual differences not only create a split within the individual but a breach between self and others. Neither the group nor the individual can grow and develop fully without the other. There is no way to realize the full possibilities in group life as long as one person is rejected, minimized, ignored, or treated as an inferior or outcast. To the extent that there is malice toward one person, ill-will and ill-feeling spread. Every person in the group is affected and is powerless to channel available resources into creative expression. One cannot carry evil thoughts, feelings, and intentions without at the same time being deterred and restrained in creative purposes of the self. One, therefore, must live through and work out one's state of rejecting or being rejected before group life can contain a depth of spirit, devotion, and authentic communality. The personal issues and disputes in the challenge of the individual confronting the group must first be met. Otherwise, the split in the group prevents each person from deriving a sense of integrity and wholeness. Only by learning to live with the deviant one, by recognizing that person's right to be and respecting the issues or problems created, can a high level of group living be realized. The personal matters must be settled first. Social or group life then follows.

We are dissatisfied with the meaningless motions, habits, and goals of modern life and the estrangement that results from impersonal study and attempts to understand rather than living imminently in the requirements or challenges of each situation.

We live in an age of analysis, yet it is never the "why" that really matters. The "why" explains; it does not inspire or create life. The "why" may help one prepare for or soften a situation, but it is not part of the real battle for truth. It is not the living experience but only an indirect substitute. The person who accepts life as a whole does not need to measure or understand or know why. It is the reality that matters. Not why it exists, but that it exists. Not why I suffer, but that I suffer. Not why I feel empty and cold and lonely, but that I am lonely and cold and afraid. Not why I am joyous and loving, but that I feel joy and love. Not why my spirit runs with the wind, but that I have suddenly awakened to an alive beauty that I have never experienced before. Not why I must die, but dying itself. The crucial moments of life do not contain a why, but only the reality that men and women are constructed in the way they are.

The supreme fact of existence is the reality itself, the experience—*this* illness, *this* conflict, *this* ecstasy, *this* life, *this* death, *this* moment transcending other moments. It is *this* realm of human experience, of immediate personal existence, whether in love or solitude, whether in suffering or despair, in which the self grows. It is not possible "to understand" while experiencing in an integrated way. Understanding of experience comes later, but it is incidental to experience itself. Kenneth Patton expresses a similar conviction in the following excerpt:

> Words, our own or another's, can never be more than a commentary upon living experience. Reading can never be substituted for living. What do I understand about a tree? I have climbed into the branches and felt the trunk sway in the winds, and I have hidden among the leaves like an apple. I have lain among the branches and ridden them like another bough, and I have torn the skin of my hands and the cloth of my trousers climbing up and down the harsh bark. I have peeled away the skin of the willow and fondled the white, sweet wood, and my ax has bitten through the pure fibers, and my saw laid bare the yearly rings and the heart-wood. Through the microscope I have copied out the traceries of the cells, and I have shaken out the rootlets like hair upon my hand; and I have chewed the gum and curled my tongue around the syrup, and shredded the wood fibers with my teeth. I have lain among the autumn leaves and my nostrils drank the smoke of their sacrifice. I have planed the yellow lumber and driven in the nails, and polished the smooth drift-wood with my palm.
>
> Within me now there is a grainyness, a leafiness, a confluence of roots and branches, forests above and afar off, and a light soil made of a thousand years of their decay, and

this whisper, this memory of fingers and nostrils, the fragile leaf-budding shivering within my eyes. What is my understanding of trees if it is not this reality lying behind these poor names? (7)

Many efforts to direct, predict, or control are in reality flights from experience or forms of self-denial. In actuality man is not predictable; man is forever impermanent. Though every person exists in a substantial way, new avenues of being and expression are continually available—not only because there are many ways in which the individual can develop potentialities but also because there are unpredictable forces in the universe and in other people that will influence development and experience. No matter how genuine a relationship may be, there will always be stresses and storms to bring unexpected words, to make one impotent and afraid, to make one feel the terribleness of not being able to count on the other person, to create the despairing feeling that breaks in love can never be repaired. But one lives and loves, and suffers and forgets, and begins again—perhaps thinking that this time, this new time, is to be permanent. But man is not permanent and man is not predictable.

Experiences of mystery and the unexpected do not occur because the person wishes or wills them. Every person is born with certain potentials and predispositions, and in fulfilling these tendencies choices are made. But the ultimate realities of living and growing and dying are a mystery. At times, the individual can choose to be or not be, to grow as a self or to develop a pseudo-self by wearing masks and incorporating ghosts. But the question of free choice and self-determination becomes relevant only if the growing self is severely denied or threatened with disapproval or rejection; or if it is confronted with an issue, challenge, question, or problem. Not all human situations, however, are confrontations and not every act of the self grows out of challenge. In most cases, development of the self is spontaneous, with the individual naturally using whatever resources are available.

The way in which I am constructed, the fact that I am a particular individual, limits me but at the same time enables me to experience in unique ways. The evolution of the self is an act of self-creation, not the accumulating of insight and understanding. This fundamental truth of the self can be realized only if the individual is willing and courageous enough to follow to some natural conclusion this moment of experience, this conviction, this ideal, this living encounter, this facing of the unknown and to participate with total commitment of the self. Such expression, such passion for life, may emerge in written, spoken, graphic, or aesthetic forms; in relation or in isolation; in I-Thou encounters; and in silent, inner experience. Not *a priori* theories, principles, or techniques, but rather a compassionate willingness is required—the courage to live before the fact, before the understanding, before any rational support or certainty, to live the moment to its natural peak and conclusion, and to accept with dignity whatever joy, grief, misfortune, or unexpectedness occurs. In this way, I am open to life, both within and without. I bring my full self into each transaction. Through the experience of my senses, through the process of risking and choosing, I find the courage to act on the basis of my intuition, judgment, and vision. I am growing with the freedom and integrity of my own self (8).

A friend of mine, who worked in a residential hospital in Northville, Michigan, met the children who had been placed there in just this open existential sense. She shared one of these relationships with me:

> One day Mark came into the playroom, looked at me and said, "There is a very ugly song going through my head, through my head, all the time." When asked to tell more about it, he said it was about the Muscle Man and he sang several bars. He continued, "It really is such a bad song, and it gives me so much trouble. Would you take me for a walk up our back road and sing to me about The Silvery Moon, to see if I can get rid of such a bad song?" With hand pressed tight in mine we walked among the beautiful autumn coloring. Everywhere the reds and yellows and golden browns surrounded us and at each step I was urged to sing: "Please sing again The Silvery Moon." Soon I was joined by a small voice and we continued our walk. After some minutes I felt the small hand slip from mine, and the feet that were heavily trudging became light, and Mark ran ahead and called back to me,

> > "The day is bea-u-ti-ful,
> > It is blue up there
> > And blue down here
> > I am up there
> > I am everywhere
> > Where it is blue.
> > The day is beau-ti-ful!"

Mark slipped back to my side and continued,

"The sky is blue and not black
The wind is soft and not hard
The clouds are white and not black
Sech a bea-u-ti-ful day
No more doggone ugly songs
Going round and round in my head."

The unfolding of this relationship is an experience of mystery between two selves, each responsible for their own destiny and yet related in a genuine way. My friend awakened the potential for new life in Mark. Her song came from inner powers that were also aroused in Mark. By "singing" to each other the powers of the self were kept alive and a life of ecstasy and joy was created.

Ultimately, I am not responsible for any other person. I participate freely and fully in life with others. I immerse myself in their world. I listen to catch the meaning, to hear the tone, to see the facial expression or body gesture. I support and affirm the flow of life that is there, the creation of words and silences, the fulfillment of the poem or melody. I speak to accentuate my presence. I respond with my whole being—mind, body, and spirit. I share what is current, what is alive in me. But, in the end, each of us finds our own path, chooses our own direction, and selects our own resources. Each of us takes responsibility for our feelings, ideas and decisions. Each of us creates our own selves.

Now when I meet with others I am no longer concerned with helping or curing them—not as a professional worker with theories and systems and rubrics and techniques. I am not even concerned with trying to understand, but only with being with the other person—as a human being who is willing to let imagination and comprehension, mental capabilities and compassion, mingle freely and to let the destiny of two lives proceed within the mystery and unpredictable nature of two growing selves engaged in immediate personal experience.

REFERENCES

1.   Dickens, Charles. *Hard Times.* Greenwich, Conn.: Fawcett Publications, 1966, p. 266.

2. Wordsworth, William. *Poetical Works*, Vol. 2. Boston: Hurd & Houghton, 1877, p. 189.

3. Maslow, A. H. *Religions, Values, and Peak Experiences*. Columbus: Ohio State University Press, 1964, p. 59.

4. Bucke, Richard M. *Cosmic Consciousness*. New York: E. P. Dutton & Co., 1901, pp. 325–329.

5. Guerard, Albert. *Bottle in the Sea*. Cambridge: Harvard University Press, 1954, pp. 154, 155.

6. Franck, Frederick. *The Zen of Seeing*. New York: Vintage Books, 1973, p. 3.

7. Patton, Kenneth L. *Man's Hidden Search*. Boston: Meeting House Press, 1954, pp. 18, 19.

8. Moustakas, Clark. *Finding Yourself, Finding Others*. Englewood Cliffs, N.J.: Prentice-Hall, 1974.

CHAPTER 3

CREATIVITY and CONFORMITY

MANY TIMES IN MY LIFE I have been faced with a dilemma that, after much internal struggle and deliberation, turned out to be illusory. Again and again I discovered that only one pathway was open, that there was only one way to go—a way that grew out of myself. The problem turned out to be not one of resolving a situation that called for a choice between unsatisfactory alternatives, but rather a question of bringing into being what already existed within myself; that is, it required bringing into being my own identity as it related to the challenge of a crucial situation. It is this experience of expressing and actualizing one's individual identity in an integrated form, in communion with one's self, with nature, and with other persons that I call creative.

Every facet of the universe, each man, woman, child, each plant and animal, the clouds and heavenly bodies, the wind and the sand and stars, each object, each space, even bits of gravel and broken stone, each item of nature, contains its own particular identity, its own unique form, its own special existence. Every aspect of nature and life attains a living unity through its relation to other identities and forms.

Growth of individual identity in open relatedness; creation of being in vital experiences with other beings; ingestion of meaning, feeling, belief, and value, within a unique self—this is the challenging responsibility and essential creativity in all life. Martin Buber expresses the indelible creativity of man as follows:

> Every person born into this world represents something new, something that never existed before, something original and unique. It is the duty of every person . . . to know . . . that there has never been anyone like him in the world, for if there had been someone like him, there would have been no need for him to be in the world. Every single man is a new thing in the world and is called upon to fulfill his particularity in this world (1).

Each real self maintains a certain substance, consistency, and autonomy, while at the same time evolving insights, meanings, and integrations. Whatever a person says or does, however alienated, detached, and unrelated he or she may become, there remains within the person forever an entirely unique and particular substance that is intact and inviolate. This substance can be recognized and called forth in encounters with other persons or forms in the universe.

To be creative means to experience life in one's own way, to perceive from one's own person, to draw upon one's own resources, capacities, roots. It means facing life directly and honestly; experiencing all of one's feelings: grief, joy, suffering, pain, struggle, conflict, and, finally, inner solitude.

The creator must often be in the world completely alone, finding the source of new life and a sense of direction within the self. According to Theodore Reik, Freud's essential creativity was his talent for searching within.

> . . . What will forever separate Freud's way from that of other psychoanalysts . . . is that his discoveries were made by himself. They were the triumph of a mind in search of itself, which, in reaching its aims, discovered the laws governing the emotional processes of all minds. We learn these discoveries with the help of books and lectures; we make them again, rediscover them, when we are in the process of analysis—that is, when we are analyzed or when we analyze others. Our psychoanalytic institutes seem to be unaware of the fact that being analyzed cannot compete in experience value with unearthing these insights oneself. . . . Nothing said to us, nothing we can learn from others, reaches us so deep as that which we find in ourselves (3).

Creativity is a process that expresses itself in unique and varying forms. It includes the capacity to mourn death and celebrate life, permitting thought, feeling, spirit to flow freely, allowing inner scenes to come into awareness and form new life. Creativity is a turning point awakened in times of challenge or crisis, involving an unknown and unpredictable path, in which there is a particular focus, concentration, exertion, or unfolding as the individual shapes new ways of being and becoming, as the individual engages in new actions and creates new life.

In the creative experience, every moment is unique and contains the potential for original expression. There are two basic requirements: that the person be direct, honest, and consistent, and that the person feel a genuine devotion to life. Creativity attains a meaningful, concrete form in a particular and unique relation. The branches of a tree stretch out expansive and free, maintaining a basic identity, an essential uniqueness in color, form, and pattern. They stand out in contrast to the fixed nature of the trunk. Yet one does not actually see the treeness of a tree without recognizing its essential harmony, its wholeness, and its unity. Each living being attains an identity and remains a living creation within a genuine whole, within an organic communion.

An experience of unusual communion is recorded by Kelman in his essay "Communing and Relating":

> I was sitting in an isolated spot on a log late one afternoon watching the brilliance of the setting sun behind the volcanoes. At that hour the lake surface was like glass and no one was on it. Not a leaf stirred. The only occasional sound, as external evidence of movement, was of a bird in flight. I do not know how long I had been sitting there when to my left, about fifty yards away, down a path, soundlessly, in their bare feet and in their native costume, came a father and his three-year-old son. They were holding hands. At the lake shore the father lifted the little boy into a boat and then got in beside him. They sat there motionless until it was almost dark. The father lifted the little boy out, took his hand, and walked up the path until they were lost to my view.
>
> Throughout I heard not a sound, saw no expressions on the face of either indicating that they were talking to one another or had even turned to look at one another. How long they or I sat there, or how much time elapsed between my arrival and my return up the path to the village, I cannot say. By the clock it might have been several hours. Feeling-wise it was a moment and eternity (4).

Not all relatedness emerges from a sense of harmony and communion. It sometimes begins with an issue, or conflict, or sense of deviation, or separateness. This was my experience on a cold, blustery day. It was a severe winter, which exceeded records for frigid temperatures, ice formations, and accumulations of snow. The cold, noisy violence of a raging wind kept me indoors. After almost two days of internment, I began to feel dull and almost completely insensible to the children's play and other events going on around me. Everything seemed colorless and toneless.

I felt trapped by the violent storm outside. The wind came swaggering through the walls and lashed against the windows, reverberating the panes, and echoing throughout the house. Screaming, fluttering sounds came through the weather stripping of the doors. Yet these auditory vibrations barely entered my center of awareness. I had been taught that the safest place in a blizzard was the warm comfort of home. And this had been my retreat for almost two days, not out of choice, but from tradition and fear. I was annoyed that a wild and fitful wind had forced me into an asylum and that I had conformed in the ordinary and intelligent way.

But something was wrong. The household scenes were gloomy. I felt the lethargy and boredom of a static life. The more I thought about my situation, the more restless I became. A growing inner feeling surged within me, and I decided to face the wind. I had never been in a blizzard before by choice, but in that moment I decided to enter the turbulence outside. Immediately, I experienced an exhilarating and exciting feeling. I stood before the bitter, cold, turbulent flow of wind, a wind that was inciting retreat and withdrawal in every direction. Momentarily I was stung and pushed back. I hesitated, uncertain whether I could move forward. It was a tremendous challenge. Holding my ground, I stood in the way of the wind. We met head-on. I knew for the first time the full meaning of a severe wind. I felt it in every pore of my body, but realized I would not retreat. I stood firm, and gradually, slowly, I began to move forward in spite of the violent, shattering gusts that emerged repeatedly to block my path. Tears fell down my face. It was a painful experience but at the same time wonderfully refreshing and joyous. It was cold, yet I was warmed by a tremendous surge of emotion. I felt radiant and alive as I continued my journey. As the wind met me and moved me, I became aware of the whole atmosphere—like a powerful dynamo; crackling, crunching, clanging noises everywhere; a rushing, swaying, churning turbulence; a world charged with electric fury. For the first time in my life I truly understood the meaning of a blizzard.

All about me were shining elements and sharp, penetrating sounds that I could see, and hear, and feel without effort. It was an awesome feeling, witnessing the wild turbulence. Everything was charged with life and beauty. The meeting with the wind revived me and restored me to my own resourcefulness. I felt an expansive and limitless energy.

I returned home. Everything took on a shining light and a spark of beauty. I played ecstatically with my children, with a burst of enthusiasm and excitement. I seemed to be inexhaustible. I made repairs, painted, helped with the evening meal, assisted with the children's baths and bedtime, and spent a joyous evening reading and conversing with my wife. Out of the tumultuous experience, I found new joy in life, new energy, uniqueness, and beauty. I had conquered my lethargy and discovered a lively affinity in everything I touched. Everything that had been dull and commonplace took on a living splendor. I realized how out of the wild, confused, turbulent experience came a sense of inner exaltation, peace, symmetry, and a recognition of the vital manifestations of life; how out of the initial conflict came a sense of individual aliveness and a feeling of harmony and relatedness to a raging wind.

For me it was clear that in the creative process the person is fully immersed in the experience, is lost as a separate being yet remains absolutely related to life, whether that life is expressed in poetry, or dance or music or an idea, or in meditation or silence, or even in encountering a raging wind. One lets go of the ordinary, the safe and familiar, of extraneous rules, of the system, and while the conscious, controlling side is dropped, the most distinguished, undisclosed characteristics of the self shine forth. Then the individual is not determined by convention and routine, but by an unusual reality, by open senses that see for the first time.

Frederick Franck points firmly to the value that inspires the poetic form: "In this twentieth century, to stop rushing around, to sit quietly on the grass, to switch off the world and come back to the earth, to allow the eye to see a willow, a bush, a cloud, a leaf, is 'an unforgetable experience' " (5). 4

Creativity is not adaptation or production. It always involves a solemn pact between one's self and others or between one's self and the raw materials of nature and life. It is a pure form of self/other relatedness. It is a way of seeing patterns or connections among discrete parts, a way of relating the unique and the universal. However different, strange, and unordinary one's way may appear to others, when it is a genuine self living and growing, it is also authentically related to life.

Maslow in his study of the creativity of self-actualizing people concluded:

> I first had to change my ideas about creativity as soon as I began studying people who were positively healthy, highly

evolved and matured, self-actualizing. I had first to give up my stereotyped notion that health, genius, talent and productivity were synonymous. A fair proportion of my subjects, though healthy and creative in a special sense . . . were not productive in the ordinary sense, nor did they have great talent or genius, nor were they poets, composers, inventors, artists or creative intellectuals.

Furthermore, I soon discovered that I had, like most other people, been thinking of creativeness in terms of products, and secondly, I had unconsciously confined creativeness to certain conventional areas only of human endeavor, unconsciously assuming that *any* painter, *any* poet, *any* composer was leading a creative life. . . . I learned that a first-rate soup is more creative than a second-rate painting, and that, generally, cooking or parenthood or making a home could be creative while poetry need not be; it could be uncreative (6).

What I am pointing to is something altogether unconditioned and transcendent of all effort, motive, or determination. It is an ultimate, universal, concrete reality that is individual yet related to life, harmonious yet discordant, congruent yet dissimilar. The creative cannot be scaled down to products, to facts or observable data. It rides on the horizons and fills the heavens. It is incomparable and can never be subsumed under categories of production, definition, and logic.

The power to create life is a human capacity that exists in every person. It can never be totally destroyed for in principal the decision to be alive and assertive is within the individual's scope at all times. The presence of the self, the valuing of one's own being, ensures an awakening, a blending of inner and outer, an awareness of who I am, what I believe, a clear sense of my own feeling and thinking and an implicit faith in my own experience to guide me and move me forward in my growth. This valuing of the self is essential if life is to be fresh, spontaneous, vital, and alive. Then each day is a new beginning, an anticipation, an unfolding.

The valuing of myself is precisely the source of my power, the unique strength that no one can take away—for in the ultimate moments my dialogue, my communion with myself, affirms me and enables me to continue to be a particular person who stands out from all others.

Our songs come from the power of being, the source of unique potential and strength that exists within each of us. When we speak to our powers, when we affirm them, then they know we

6

are telling them something (*7*). There is an awakening, a response, a return of life. Our powers hear our own songs; they want to listen. If you don't sing your own songs, if you don't play your own music and speak your own words, if you don't live your own silences, then the powers within you will not know where to find you. They will not know how to work for you.

The creative process emerges within vital experience, in the flow of real feelings, in an intimate relation to nature, to oneself, and to other selves.

When a person's involvement in a situation is based on appearances, expectations, or the standards of others; when the individual acts in a conventional manner or according to prescribed roles and functions; when he or she is concerned with status and approval, growth as a creative self is impaired. When the individual is conforming, following, imitating, being like others, movement is increasingly in the direction of self-alienation. Such a person fears issues and controversies, fears standing out or being different. The person does not think through experience to find the value or meaning, does not permit a spontaneous flow of perceptions to some natural conclusion. Such a person avoids directly facing disputes, becomes anxious in situations that require self-awareness and self-discovery, becomes increasingly similar, and eventually erases real identity and uniqueness. Maslow points out that the only way such a person can achieve safety, order, lack of threat, and lack of anxiety is through orderliness, predictability, control, and mastery (*8*). If the conformist can proceed into the future on the basis of "well-tried" rules, habits, and modes of adjustment that have worked in the past (and that are believed to be workable in the future), he or she feels safe. But when a new situation is faced that does not clearly define appropriate behavior, does not make explicit what is acceptable, then the person experiences deep anxiety and despair.

Gradually, conforming people lose touch with themselves, with their own real feelings. They are unable to experience life in a genuine way, yet they suffer inwardly and experience the guilt of not fulfilling their potentials. The torment remains because they cannot get rid of themselves and they are not satisfied with living dishonestly.

In conformity, life has no meaning for there is no true basis for existence. Cut off from real wishes and capacities, the individual experiences no fulfillment and no sense of authentic relatedness. The person's primary goal is to achieve safety and status, to overcome natural desires, and through acquisition and control to gain a victory over natural surroundings. Separated from nature and others yet appearing to be in harmony, the person takes cues from the designated authority figures. A young woman in psychotherapy recognized this pattern.

> So you have to put everything out . . . as a question, you know. Because he's the one who knows and we're the ones who don't know. You can't (pause) you're sort of stepping onto his territory if *you* start giving out with pronouncements of facts. You see, what you're doing is you're competing, you're being disrespectful. You're moving into his position which—you just *don't do* that. . . . And I know that very well, but how I know it or why I know it—you see, I don't know it as intellectual concept—I just *know* it. My father didn't allow anybody but himself to be the lawgiver and statement maker. . . . And a lot of those things I know, I don't know in words, I just *know* (9).

Another way in which conformity is developed is through the labeling of people. In labeling, the individual is fixed so that reality is not experienced or known. Often the person loses touch with who he or she is and becomes the label. When we call others dumb or stupid or lazy, we are stamping them with that characteristic just as directly as if we were clubbing and severely injuring them. Labels are missiles that undermine and restrict or pressure a person to stray toward conforming to other's definitions and standards.

The conformist has been forced into denying the self, not as the result of valid limits but because of frequent experiences of being rejected or of being rewarded for adopting other people's labels, definitions, and expectations. A distinction must be made here between natural limits and imposed limitations. *Limits* provide the structure through which individual identity emerges and grows (10).[7] They enable the individual to use capacities within a defined structure and are meaningful as the inherent requirements of a situation. *Limitations* are induced and imposed from without and are external and extraneous. They are blocks and deterrents to growth and hinder creative emergence.

Conforming persons do not use their own resources, their own experiences, but take direction from experts, authority figures, and traditional guides. Somewhere along the way conformists have given up their actual identity and submerged themselves in the acceptable group modes. Conformists might be quite comfortable from the standpoint of material security and social relationships—as long as they stay within the standard patterns and expectations—but they have lost touch with their own uniqueness, the sources of inner life that would move them toward creativity and individuality and turn them away from the usual reward system. Thus, the conforming person is cut off from self-resources that would inspire autonomy and real growth. Having been rejected as independent selves because they veered from what was acceptable and valued by those in authority, they also have come to reject themselves.

This tragedy is expressed beautifully in the following passage from a patient of Karen Horney's:

> How is it possible to lose a self? The treachery, unknown and unthinkable, begins with our secret psychic death in childhood—if and when we are not loved and are cut off from our spontaneous wishes.
>
> Oh, they "love" him, but they want him or force him or expect him to be different! Therefore he must be *unacceptable*. He himself learns to believe it and at last even takes it for granted. He has truly given himself up. No matter now whether he obeys them, whether he clings, rebels, or withdraws—his behavior, his performance is all that matters. His center of gravity is in "them," not in himself—yet if he so much as noticed that, he'd think it natural enough. And the whole thing is entirely plausible; all invisible, automatic, and anonymous!
>
> This is the perfect paradox. Everything looks normal; no crime was intended; there is no corpse, no guilt. All we can see is the sun rising and setting as usual. But what has happened? He has been rejected, not only by them but by himself. (He is actually without a self.) What has he lost? Just the one true and vital part of himself: His own yes-feeling, which is his very capacity for growth, his root system (11).

Conforming people are programmed to perceive in a certain way, in the way that adults view things; the adult with authority, of course, perceives correctly. The process begins at an early age and gradually, through repetitive conditioning and reward or fear of punishment and rejection, they begin to behave in approved ways without being aware of conforming. They take on a life that is outlined and determined by others rather than an identity based on real experience. Inner feelings are no longer trusted, and since one cannot actually make another's feelings one's own, the individual learns mechanically or automatically to make the proper gestures or facial expressions. A smile is not a smile; joy is not joy; and sadness is not sadness. The body and spirit are frozen and the movements of the face and body are properly placed in the appearance of the appropriate emotions. Conforming persons are anesthetic; they are embedded in a world without color, without excitement, without risk or danger, without mystery—in a word, without life (12). //

We deny the existence of children as individuals through the use of competitive standards, through imposing our judgments of what is appropriate or valued. Jules Henry's report of the destructive consequences of competition and the breeding of hatred in our schools is a frightening, devastating document. Henry presents an incident that occurred during a fifth-grade arithmetic lesson. Boris is at the blackboard attempting to reduce a fraction to its lowest terms. He is performing for the teacher and class and is having trouble reducing the fraction. The teacher suggests that he "think." There is a great deal of heaving up and down and waving of hands by other children who are all frantic to correct Boris. Finally, the teacher gives up with Boris and calls on Peggy, who quickly gives the right answer. Henry concludes:

> Thus Boris' failure has made it possible for Peggy to succeed; his depression is the price of her exhilaration, his misery the occasion of her rejoicing. This is the standard condition of the American elementary school. . . . Somebody's success has been bought at the cost of our failure. To a Zuni, Hopi, or Dakota Indian, Peggy's performance would seem cruel beyond belief, for competition, the wringing of success from somebody's failure, is a form of torture. . . . Yet Peggy's action seems natural to us; and so it is. How else would you run our world? And since all but the brightest children have the constant experience that others succeed at their expense, they cannot but develop an inherent tendency to hate—to hate the success of others, to hate others who are successful, and to be determined to prevent it. Along with this, naturally, goes the hope that others will fail (13).

12

Conforming people do not actualize their potentials, do not realize what they can do. Cut off from their own desires and resources, they are not free to make choices based on a philosophy of growth, on a developing meaning of life, and on human values. They may sometimes appear to be persons with great sureness, with precise and emphatic ways, confident persons who take possession of themselves and others. But these are attributes coordinated to the conventional views of success and often internalized so strongly that it is difficult to discern the real from the counterfeit.

Much of the misery in the world today, the serious emotional problems and conflicts, results from efforts to fit people into conventional modes and from strivings for success, status, and power—goals that offer no intrinsic values or satisfactions and that contribute to a meaningless existence. Failure to grow as a self results from a failure to maintain a unique identity in significant or crucial situations and an inability to meet others directly and honestly. Following traditional patterns and external guides, basing one's life on competitive strivings and the rewards of the marketplace, modeling oneself after people in authority or with high status, individuals no longer know who they are. They do not mean what they say and do not do what they believe and feel. Responding with surface or approved thoughts, they learn to use devious and indirect ways and to base their behavior on the standards and expectations of others. They move increasingly toward falsehood, fakery, and pretense. Their values and convictions emerge not from real experiences, but from a feeling of danger and anxiety, from a fear of not keeping pace, a fear of being minimized, and a desire to be protected from rejection and attack. Cut off from themselves, they are unable to have honest experiences with others or commune with nature. They base their lives on appearances and deceptions and on manipulation and control. Without any deep and growing roots, they move in accordance with external signals. They do not know their place in the world, where they are or who they are. Having lost touch with spontaneity, with real interests, they are unable to be direct, genuine, loving human beings.

To the degree that the individual strives to attain similarity or congruity, to the degree that actions are geared toward being popular or victorious or approved of, to the degree that individuals model themselves after others, they fail to grow as selves, fail to develop unique identities, fail to grow as creative beings with desires and capacities, with lives that are genuinely related to others.

I have had the experience of living in a false world, of being disturbed and disabled by the manipulation and cruelty that is sometimes strongly part of my life. One day I was deeply depressed by the severe criticisms a colleague had received—a person who was living his life in an honest and truthful sense, attempting to express his unique interests through his work. I felt saddened when I realized how he had suffered, how he had struggled to maintain a personal and creative identity, a genuine existence and relatedness. I felt especially sensitive to pretense and surface behavior, as though nothing were real. A numbness settled in at the center of my thoughts and feelings. That night even the children were unable to shake my grief and sadness. In their own spontaneous, unknowing ways, they tugged and pulled at me to draw me into life, but for me there remained only suffering in the world.

After the children had gone to bed, I decided to go for a walk. The night was dark, filled with black clouds. Large white flakes of snow fell on and around me. The night was silent and serene. Suddenly, without understanding in any way, I experienced a transcendental beauty in the white darkness. It was difficult to walk on the glazed surface, but as I continued I felt drawn to the black, inky streaks embedded in the ice. Dark, wavy lines, partly covered by snow, spread out in grotesque forms. I knelt down, touching the black, irregular patterns. Immediately I felt a chill, but at the same time the ice began melting as my fingers touched it.

My inward heaviness lifted, and I was restored to a new capacity for exertion and endurance. I realized how, out of broken roots and fibers, in a genuine encounter with natural resources, it is possible to develop new strength and conviction. I realized how the self can be shattered in surface and false meetings when surrounded by intensive pressures to conform, and how in communion with nature the self can reach a new dimension of optimism and a new recognition of the creative way of life. Possibilities for unique and unusual meetings exist everywhere. We need only reach out in authentic ways to come face to face with creation.

REFERENCES

1. Buber, Martin. *Hasidism and Modern Man.* Ed. and tr. by Maurice Friedman. New York: Horizon Press, 1958, pp. 139, 140.

2. Reik, Theodore. *The Search Within.* New York: Farrar, Strauss & Cudahy, 1956, pp. 263, 264.

3. Kelman, Harold. "Communing and Relating. Part II, Examples: General and Clinical." *American Journal of Psychoanalysis* 19 (1959): 74–75.

4. Franck, Frederick. *The Zen of Seeing.* New York: Vintage Books, 1973, p. xx.

5. Maslow, A. H. *Toward A Psychology of Being.* Princeton, N.J.: D. Van Nostrand Co., 1962, pp. 127, 128.

6. Basso, Keith. *Cibecue Apache.* New York: Holt, Rinehart and Winston, 1970.

7. Maslow, A. H. "Emotional Blocks to Creativity." *Journal of Individual Psychology* 14 (1958): 51–56.

8. Will, Otto, and Cohen, Robert H. "A Report of A Recorded Interview in the Course of Psychotherapy." *Psychiatry* 16 (1953): 268.

9. Moustakas, Clark. *Psychotherapy With Children: The Living Relationship.* New York: Harper Bros., 1959, pp. 9–11.

10. Horney, Karen. "Finding the Real Self." *American Journal of Psychoanalysis* 9 (1949): 3–7.

11. Moustakas, Clark. *Personal Growth.* Cambridge, Mass.: Howard A. Doyle Publishing Co., 1969, p. 4.

12. Henry, Jules. *Culture Against Man.* New York: Random House, 1963, pp. 295–296.

Chapter 4

Confrontation and Encounter

ONLY BRIEFLY ARE WE KNOWN in the deepest regions of ourselves, yet within these brief encounters we experience the value of recognition and communion. When we are in trouble, when we have made mistakes, when we are at odds with the world, when we have futile visions and dreams, the caring for another person enables us to remain alive in our own growth, to struggle with issues and problems, to find a way to fulfill our hopes and aspirations.

Two ways in which we establish significant bonds with others are the confrontation and the encounter. The *creative confrontation* is a meeting between persons who are involved in a conflict or controversy and who remain together, face-to-face, until their feelings of divisiveness are expressed and clarified, until there is acceptance on a person-to-person level and respect for differences. In contrast, the *encounter* is a sudden, spontaneous meeting of harmony and mutuality, a feeling of being within the life of another person while at the same time maintaining one's own identity and individuality.

THE CONFRONTATION

In our meetings with others conflicts arise and irritations grow until we no longer wish to continue to live with each other in the same ways. Then, either the relationship will deteriorate or the persons will face each other and struggle with the issues and problems. The confrontation is not an intellectually planned session that requires an audience and a referee. It is a private, intimate conflict between persons that happens, often spontaneously and unexpectedly, when a crisis arises in a relationship and the persons realize that they must either reach a new level of life together or face the consequences of a broken relationship.

The confrontation may be brief or it may be of long duration, depending on the depth and intensity of the dispute. It requires that the persons remain together until there is a resolution of feelings. The individuals may terminate the confrontation, still at odds as far as the issue is concerned, but not at odds with each other. This is the important point to realize—that each person must be free to maintain his or her own identity if a relationship is to have any valid meaning.

The confrontation is a way to deeper intimacy and relatedness, to authentic life between persons. The persons must be courageous enough to live through the unknown factors in the confrontation, trusting enough to let the breach heal through silent presence and communion when words and dialogue fail, strong enough to maintain a caring and respect for each other whatever else may be cancelled out in the issue or dispute. The persons never lose sight of the fact that each is seeking in his or her own way, however fragmentary or futile or destructive it may appear, to find an authentic existence, to find a life of meaning and value, and to express the truth.

In the classroom confrontation, the child must have the right to be in disagreement with the teacher. Paradoxical as this seems, when persons can openly disagree, it is possible for them to establish genuine bonds. When the teacher forces the child to submit through repetitious phrases and commands, through conditioning, belittling, group pressures, brainwashing devices, through the intimidation of an artificial curriculum, the child soon realizes that the only acceptable way is the path of conformity. Increasingly, in such an atmosphere, children become insensitive to their own selves and unresponsive to their own experience. They become numb to criticism and rebuke, develop a suspicious and mechanical defense against further attacks, and come to be unfeeling in their associations with teachers.

In my visits to classrooms, I initially find children eager to share their experiences, their knowledge and skills. In one second-grade classroom when the children saw the principal and me enter the room, they were immediately eager to read to us. A child, with a smiling face and shining eyes, was called on to read. She sighed with joy as she began, "Casey Joins the Circus." Apparently, she had learned that a good reader varies her tone of voice, reads loud enough for others to hear, and reads fluently. Wanting to make an impression, wanting to get the praise of her teacher and classmates, she hurried through the paragraph assigned to her. But something was wrong. Mrs. Bell interrupted the child. She pushed the book away from the child's face and said in a slow deliberate voice, hovering over the child, "You are reading carelessly. That's not showing respect for what is printed on the page. It's not showing respect for our visitors or the other boys and girls. You are making sense, but you simply are not reading the words in the book. I've told you about this before, Betsy. Now you go back and read what's printed there so we can all follow you." The child returned to the beginning of the paragraph, but something had happened. She had no direct, open way of relating to her audience. The staring, judging faces of the other children frightened her. She read in a reluctant manner, pronouncing words haltingly. There was a weak, muffled quality in her voice. She had been hurt. She was no longer certain. She completed the reading and slumped wearily into her chair.

The real tragedy was not in the critical words of the teacher or in the subdued child, but in the fact that communication was not on a person-to-person basis, not on a level of equality. There was the teacher as law-giver and statement-maker, as the one in authority. There was the adult voice, belittling, shaming, humiliating the child into exact reading. The teacher used the visitors and the other children to prove her point and impress the child. She did not keep the issue between herself and the child, where it belonged. And it was all done matter-of-factly, as professional duty. It was all impersonal and without feeling.

There was also the subdued, frightened voice of the child. Besty read and read and read and read, every word in the paragraph. Was it worth killing that spontaneity, that joy, that wonder in a little girl's voice as she tried to please her audience, for the sake of a word-by-word conformity to a printed page?

Betsy was not just a reader, not merely a machine producing and transmitting sounds. There beside me was a human being. She was really there, wanting to see her teacher smile, a gesture that would make her feel valued even though she made mistakes. But this teacher did not offer the child sympathy, respect, sensitivity, or affirmation. Instead, she performed a function. The confrontation never got beyond the initial reproof. Oh, yes, Besty went through the motion of reading, but *she* was no longer there. She could not face her teacher as an open person any more.

No individual is perfect. We all make mistakes. But to commit a wrong, to lower the dignity of a child and not be aware that that dignity had been impaired, was much more serious than the child's skipping of words during oral reading. The real tragedy was the teacher's lack of sensitivity and awareness, her failure to recognize the child as a person.

Another powerful example of a destructive confrontation between a grown-up and a child is portrayed in D. H. Lawrence's *The Rainbow*. Here is a brief excerpt describing a father's violent attack on his daughter. The father remains unaware of the impact of his hostility on her developing sense of self and their relationship.

> He would smash into her sensitive child's world . . . her soul would almost start out of her body as her father turned on her, shouting:
> "Who's been tramplin' an' dancin' across where I've just sowed seed? I know it's you, nuisance! Can you find nowhere else to walk, but just over my seed beds? But it's like you, that is—no heed but to follow your own greedy nose . . . (1).

Ursula's father had been shocked to find her footprints zigzagging across his field but Ursula was more completely shocked in his sudden attack on her, in his flaying and trampling on her soul. She had not wanted her footprints there. She was seeking only the green-pink flowers for her tea party. And now she stood before him dazzled with the pain and shame aroused by his vicious rejection of her.

> The sense of her own unreality hardened her like a frost. . . .
> "I'll break your obstinate little face," he said, through shut teeth, lifting his hand (1).

In that moment Ursula looked at him with absolute indifference, with that fixed glance of apparently not caring. But in her were sobs tearing her soul. "And when he had gone she would go and creep under the parlour sofa, and lie clinched in the silent, hidden misery of childhood."

Though Urusla loved her father, the violence of his confrontation hurt her indelibly, and she would carry that voice forever that bullied and tormented her—it would force her into her own world of silence and isolation.

When an adult loses sight of a child as a human being and fails to recognize the child's presence as a person, there is no reality between them, there is no relationship. This is what happens in many situations where potential growth exists between persons. The persons are lost and the discrepancy or issue becomes all that matters. The loudest voice, the strongest figure, the person in authority carries out the office of command. Gradually the child is forced into a state where feelings and senses are muffled and subdued until eventually he or she is no longer aware of what is being experienced. When people reject, humiliate, hurt, belittle, control, dominate, and brutalize others without being aware of what they are doing, there is little hope that human values will ever become the basis for living and growing.

Desensitization occurs through a process of deprivation and separation in which one is treated as an object; in which materials or skills and subject matter are more significant than persons; in which goals must be pursued regardless of the wishes, aspirations, and capacities of the persons involved; in which rationalizing, explaining, and analyzing take the place of spontaneity and natural feeling. The adult who observes, manipulates, and directs children, probes into them, writes them up, and breaks them down into specific traits of weakness and strength is actually treating the child as a thing—and the child soon learns to react as one. When children are perceived as objects, when they are regarded merely as members of a group or mass society, there is real danger that they will lose their identities as unique persons. They will then become insensitive to laughter and mimicry and sarcasm; insensitive to the range of feelings that characterize genuine human existence.

In its extreme form, what happens in everyday life to encourage dehumanization is not unlike what occurred in the death camps during World War II. The dehumanization of the prisoner of war is forcefully described by Viktor Frankl in this brief narrative based on his experiences in four concentration camps:

> At first the prisoner looked away if he saw the punishment parades of another group: he could not bear to see fellow prisoners march up and down for hours in the mire, their movements directed by blows. Days or weeks later things changed. The prisoner did not avert his eyes any more. By then his feelings were blunted, and he watched unmoved. He stood unmoved while a twelve-year-old boy was carried in who had been forced to stand at attention for hours in the snow or to work outside with bare feet because there were no

shoes for him in the camp. His toes had become frostbitten, and the doctor on duty picked off the black gangrenous stumps with tweezers, one by one. Disgust, horror and pity are emotions that our spectator could not really feel any more. The sufferers, the dying and the dead, became such commonplace sights to him after a few weeks of camp life that they could not move him any more (2).

Protesting against the dehumanization of individuals in modern societies, Norman Cousins registers this warning:

> What is happening, I believe, is that the natural reactions of the individual against violence are being blunted. The individual is being desensitized by living history. He is developing new reflexes and new responses that tend to slow up the moral imagination and relieve him of essential indignation over impersonal hurt. He is becoming casual about brutality. He makes his adjustments to the commonplace, and nothing is more commonplace in our age than the ease with which life can be smashed or shattered. The range of the violence sweeps from the personal to the impersonal, from the amusements of the crowd to the policies of nations. It is in the air, quite literally. It has lost the sting of surprise (3).

In contrast to the confrontation that does not go beyond the initial issue or conflict is the creative dispute between persons where each person is aware of the other's full legitimacy, where there is equality on a person-to-person level. In the healthy confrontation neither person loses sight of the fact that each is seeking to express the truth and to find a meaningful way to live. In a true confrontation the persons always remain persons. And because there is awareness and knowledge and sensitivity, the argument, the face-to-face struggle, follows its natural course and opens new pathways of relatedness. In times of creative confrontation, the relationship unfolds into more and more meaningful expressions of the self. Feelings are released, conflicts resolved, and a new sense of responsibility developed. In a real meeting, all dimensions and resources of the self converge, the whole being comes to grips with an impelling human conflict. In no way is either person reduced by this, but rather the individuals maintain a unique sense of self and realize the worth of honesty and directness in communication and relationships.

In the classroom, the teacher has a special challenge and responsibility. The conflict with a pupil can be the supreme test for the educator, who must face this conflict and come through it to a meaningful way of life, a life where confidence continues unshaken, even strengthened. In his essay on the education of character, Buber describes the difficulty of creative resolution of conflict between a teacher and child, as illustrated in this passage:

> He must use his own insight wholeheartedly; he must not blunt the piercing impact of his knowledge, but he must at the same time have in readiness the healing ointment for the heart pierced by it. Not for a moment may he conduct a dialectical maneuver instead of the real battle for truth. But if he is the victor he has to help the vanquished endure defeat; and if he cannot conquer the self-willed soul that faces him (for victories over souls are not so easily won), then he has to find the word of love which alone can help to overcome so difficult a situation (4).

The adult is sometimes afraid to confront a child who is hostile, caustic, or vengeful. Such an adult avoids the child until the accumulation of feelings becomes so unbearable that an explosion occurs and the adult loses control. Once the self is out of control, there is no possibility to bring about a positive resolution of the problem. But when the hateful, rejecting emotions subside, there is always hope that the adult can come to terms with the child in a positive way. The anxiety in facing an embittered, destructive child can be eliminated only by an actual confrontation with the youngster. Until we actually meet the child in an open and honest confrontation we cannot know him or her. We cannot know whether we can live with the child, whether we can face the issue and maintain our own identity.

Viewing the child solely as an immature person is a way of escaping a confrontation. Thinking of the child only as a learner who is slow or lazy or careless is a way of avoiding the feelings a controversial meeting may bring forth. Considering a child as the "other" is all part of the estrangement process, when professional and social roles separate and alienate adult and child as persons.

In the true confrontation, the external, objective framework is abandoned. The individual departs from the familiar and goes forth to an unknown meeting with the other person. The threat of anxiety, to some extent, can be controlled by avoiding the unknown, by restricting the scope of life, by remaining immersed in the familiar and not venturing out. Because this makes for stagnation, we must be determined to go forward and keep open the doors to an expanding life with others (5).

BRIAN

Something in the nature of anxiety in confronting an enraged child who has broken a limit in therapy held me for many years. Until recently I rationalized and explained away my anxiety to the point of convincing myself that to end the interview was the appropriate response to the repeated breaking of a limit. This was my way of teaching the child his responsibility to the relationship. After many such experiences, I realized, however, that I had never lived with an enraged child long enough to know what it actually means to be with a child who refuses to be denied. I had sent the child away at a time when love and understanding mattered most.

I realized one day with Brian that I had to see what existed beyond my fixed policy of terminating a meeting when it became destructive. I wondered if I could, without jeopardizing the value of our relationship, remain with a child in severe conflict until bedrock was reached; until an ultimate limit, a true dimension of the unfolding relationship, could be established and held.

Brian had been coming for weekly therapy sessions for almost a year when his intense feelings of love and hate reached a peak. For three months, each experience had begun with a sword and gun battle between us. He screamed with delight each time he "pierced or cut" me, each time he shot and killed me. When these battles were first initiated, we had agreed to keep them within a ten-minute time limit. Following the battle with me, he would proceed to shoot and kill all human and animal figures in the room. He would take a rifle and scrape to the floor all items on tables and the tops of cabinets. Often he would open the plastic paint containers and place them at the edge of a shelf, shooting at them until the paint sprayed against the walls and onto the floor. This barrage and the hostile attack had been repeated in similar pattern for thirteen weeks. Then one day we faced each other on a different interpersonal level.

The usual ten-minute battle had been completed but Brian refused to stop. He decided to use me as a target for what he called "bow and arrow" practice. I explained that there were items in the room that he could use, but that I did not wish to be his target. The following conversation took place:

MR. M: Brian, I have already explained I do not want to be used as a target. *(As I express my feeling, Brian shoots again, this time hitting my arm.)*

MR. M: Brian, that hurt. Perhaps that's what you want— to hurt me. *(Brian is about to shoot again.)*

MR. M: No, Brian. I will not permit it again. I'm going to have to insist that you give me the bow and arrows. I do not intend to let you shoot me again. *(Brian laughs nervously. With a sadistic glee in his voice, he tries to pull away, but I hold the bow firmly. He drops the arrows.)*

BRIAN: You never let me do anything. All you ever think of is No! No! No!

MR. M: Yes, I know. You think I stop you at every turn.

BRIAN: Will you play tic-tac-toe with me?

MR. M: Yes, if you'd like me to, but I saw your thought. I know what you intend doing. If you throw one more item at me, I'm going to have to do something drastic. *(The game begins. Suddenly Brian begins laughing wildly. He throws the chalk and eraser at me. He tries to run to the "out-of-bounds" area. I block his path. He picks up a pile of books and throws them.)*

MR. M: All right, Brian. Everything in the room is out of bounds for the rest of this time. You may have only this small space here. We can sit and talk or just sit.

BRIAN: You can't make me stay in this part.

MR. M: Oh, yes, I can. We've reached a point now where this is the only place we have. *(Pause.)*

BRIAN: I hate you. *(Pause.)* I could kill you.

MR. M: Yes, you really want to hurt me the way you feel I have hurt you. *(Brian slaps me.)*

MR. M: I now must hold your arms. *(Suddenly Brian completely relaxes. He lays his head on my shoulder.)*

BRIAN: You never let the baby have his bottle.

MR. M: You always had to cry and throw things before you were fed.

BRIAN: I want my bottle.

MR. M: Would you like me to rock you? *(Sitting together quietly on the floor, I rock Brian for a few minutes.)* (6)

This was a full, vital, complete experience of two persons, involving struggle, suffering, and pain—but it was also a growth experience. The limits were important not only because they provided a structure for the relationship but also because they were necessary for the child and therapist to learn to live together in harmony. Eventually Brian and I formed deep ties and the roots of a healthy relationship.

The dispute over the broken limit significantly affected the outcome of psychotherapy. When Brian returned, he greeted me with a feeling of intimacy. He plunged into new areas of conflict and openly revealed his feelings. Having lived through a significant controversy with me, having met me as a person, Brian was able to verbalize his feelings of self-doubt, to say that his parents considered him a "bad," destructive child, and to relate directly a number of crucial experiences in which he had been severely denied as a self. Thus, in spite of the apparent breach, we formed deep ties that enabled Brian to develop a sense of self-esteem, freedom to be, and a respect for the rights of others.

The life that began between us in the confrontation over limits has continued to grow and expand over many years. Brian is now a young adult, happily married and thoroughly enjoying his work. We still meet from time to time, and value in each other a way of open communication, spontaneity, unbroken trust, and a human presence and responsiveness. I believe the original confrontation was the turning point in the therapy and in our relationship. The strength, power, and love that grew out of that crisis still remains between us.

I conclude this section with a confrontation involving a strong disagreement between a teacher and a class of eighth-grade children. The situation is narrated by the teacher herself.

Mrs. Lawrence Confronts Her Group

Over a period of many months, a fairly successful teacher-indoctrination or "brainwashing" had been executed in this group on the joys of research study and the woeful disadvantages of using just one textbook for their work. But, someplace along the line another job of "thinking and speaking for yourself, expressing your own convictions" had been running a strong counter course! Like a regiment in ambush they sprang one quiet day; almost united to a man on the pleasure they would derive from having a text, a single book, with discussion questions and problem exercises, "like the other kids." Being kicked in the stomach might have been less painful to me at that moment; and to save the sinking ship and the drowning crew, I pulled out all the stops.

"Have you no appreciation of the value of looking at things more than one way? Can't you see the *fun* you could have putting ideas together from many phases of American life and from many different sources? What about the legends, literature, art, music, and dances of your people," I stormed. "Can't you draw some conclusions of your own? Must you have it crammed down your throats from the pages of one little book; and one dictating teacher." And for a final "piece de resistance," in words to this effect, or more accurately, in these very words, I said, "You are all just plain lazy! You want to be spoon fed."

Well, there was hardly a dry eye in the house, the little scene I had staged had brought about the desired effect! Proud? Well, at that moment perhaps, but still rational enough to add: "You needn't decide now what you want to do; but tomorrow I will expect you to indicate on a slip of paper if you prefer to have the textbook for the year, or if you would prefer to work together from many resources and research methods toward some meaningful insights and conclusions."

When my shaking stopped, and I sat in my empty classroom, I began thinking of the ugliness of the whole thing! This is teaching? Victory at any cost? It didn't take too long for me to realize that some of the very people who mattered most must now wonder if they really know me as an honest self. Where was the consistency of my values now?

I can't say that I knew what I was going to do about it when I walked into class the next day; in spite of the long night's struggle and post-mortem of the confrontation, but I applied, through no advanced plan of my own, the age old principle of apologizing when you know you have done something wrong. I held to my belief in the value of the resources, methods and principles we had used in the past months, but I admitted temporary irrationalism and professed that my lack of respect for their opinions was inexcusable! If it would afford them a better opportunity to state their views, and if it wasn't too late, I suggested a discussion. Everyone had something to say and the cleansing power of my words resulted in a completely different classroom atmosphere and heightened sense of group solidarity. My pleasure in being a part of this was only commensurate with the knowledge that I had learned far more than any child in the room from this experience.

THE ENCOUNTER

The encounter is a direct meeting between two persons who happen to come together. It may be an exchange of brief duration or last a long time, a meeting with a friend or a total stranger. In such a meeting there is human intimacy and depth. Although every confrontation is an encounter, not every encounter involves a dispute or controversy. Sometimes the encounter is a simple coming together of two faces or pairs of eyes, a sudden sense of knowing and being within the other, a feeling of harmony. The encounter is an immediate, imminent reality between two persons engaged in a living communion, where there is an absolute relatedness and a sense of mutuality.

The encounter is a creative experience, in which there is a dropping off of conventions, a letting go, so that one enters into the reality of a situation in terms of the conditions and requirements intrinsic to that situation. Openness, receptiveness, and relatedness are significant aspects of the encounter. There is a free and open play of attention, thought, feeling, and perception. The openness and intensity of interest may range from the grave, serious, and absorbing, to the tantalizing, playful, and fleeting.

The encounter is not a fortuitous meeting of two individuals, but rather a decisive inner experience in which something totally new is revealed, in which new horizons are opened. Martin Buber relates an encounter between an educator and a student, a vital meeting that occurred when a young teacher faced his class for the first time.

Undecided whether to issue orders immediately or to set up rules and standards of conduct, the teacher suddenly encounters a face in the crowd, a face that impresses him. It is not a beautiful face, but a real face, and it contains an expression into which the

teacher reads the question: "Who are you? Do you know something that concerns me?" I quote the passage that presents this encounter:

> In some such ways he reads the question. And he, the
> young teacher, addresses this face. He says nothing very pon-
> derous or important, he puts an ordinary introductory ques-
> tion: "What did you talk about last in geography? The Dead
> Sea? Well, what about the Dead Sea?" But there was ob-
> viously something not quite usual in the question, for the
> answer he gets is not the ordinary schoolboy answer; the boy
> begins *to tell a story.* Some months earlier he had stayed for a
> few hours on the shores of the Dead Sea and it is of this he
> tells. He adds: "Everything looked to me as if it had been
> created a day before the rest of creation." Quite unmistakably
> he had only in this moment made up his mind to talk about it.
> In the meantime his face has changed. It is no longer quite as
> chaotic as before. And the class has fallen silent. They all
> listen. The class, too, is no longer a chaos. Something has
> happened. The young teacher has started from above (7).

No matter how complicated or restricted or frightening life
appears to be, the opportunity for encounter is always present.
However heavy the pressures and responsibilities of life, there is
nothing that can prevent genuine meetings with other persons.
The possibility of encounter exists as a reality if a person is willing to make the required human commitment.

My own relationship with adults was significantly altered
through an experience with an old man—particularly my capacity
to bear pain and suffering and my sensitivity to loneliness. This
encounter involved an old man who hated himself and wanted to
die and his therapist, who desired to remain alive with him during the most devastating illness of his life (8).

I experienced totally the challenge of lonely encounter with
this old man who had come to me on the verge of suicide, believing that he had lived his life in a false and dishonest way, that he
had killed his real self long ago, and that he no longer knew what
was genuine and what was counterfeit.

Each time he came I felt that I too was sinking into total despair. Often when he wept, there were tears in my eyes too, and
when his head ached painfully, I felt the pain all the way through
me. When he paced and pulled at himself, I felt a terrible restless-

ness and agitation. My full, complete presence was not enough to alleviate his suffering, his self-lacerating expressions. I felt desolate, unable to help him find a beginning, locate a direction, discover a new pathway of relatedness to himself and others. It hurt deeply to see him grow increasingly, unbelievably tortured. He was dying before me and something within me was dying too. I could not reach him. I do not know what effort of will, what inner strivings of the heart, what forces kept me going in the face of this unendurable, mounting desolation, despair, and loneliness. I felt defeated and weakened, yet each time he came I met him squarely, honestly, directly. Each time my capacity for bearing with him seemed to be reaching a terminal point, new threads inside revived me. Somehow fresh strength flowed into me, mysteriously encouraging me and enabling me to continue. I listened to him and believed in him. I was convinced he had the power within himself to create a new life.

Suddenly he stopped coming. After some time he called to say he wanted to share something with me. When he entered, his radiant smile was like joyous music filling my office. In the interim, he had found a new source of life. In surrendering completely to his pain and loneliness, he had found an opening for each day. He had found work, creating stained glass designs, in which he could express his talents and skills.

So we sat in silence, each reveling in the birth, each warmed by a bond that emerged from deep and spreading roots in the hours of anguish and loneliness. We were no longer alone or lonely. We had found a new strength and sustenance in each other. The fundamental communion in which we suffered enabled him to get to the very depths of his experience. Perhaps at the foundation of his grief and loneliness, immediate death or immediate life were his only choices. He chose to live. From his rock-bottom loneliness a new life emerged, and a real self was restored.

Martin Buber expresses the same value in the following passage from *Hasidism and Modern Man:*

> . . . Not to help out of pity, that is, out of a sharp, quick pain which one wishes to expel, but out of love, that is, out of living with the other. He who pities does not live with the suffering of the sufferer, he does not bear it in his heart as one bears the life of a tree with all its drinking in and shooting forth and with the dream of its roots and craving of its trunk

and the thousand journeys of its branches, or as one bears the life of an animal with all its gliding, stretching, and grasping and all the joy of its sinews and its joints and the dull tension of its brain. He does not bear in his heart this special essence, the suffering of the other; rather he receives from the most external features of this suffering a sharp, quick pain, unbridgeably dissimilar to the original pain of the sufferer. And it is thus that he is moved. But the helper must live with the other, and only help that arises out of living with the other can stand before the eyes of God (9).

REFERENCES

1. Lawrence, D. H. *The Rainbow.* New York: Viking Press, 1961, pp. 220–222.

2. Frankl, Viktor F. *Man's Search for Meaning: An Introduction to Logo Therapy.* Boston: Beacon Press, 1962, pp. 19, 20.

3. Cousins, Norman. "The Desensitization of Twentieth-Century Man." *Saturday Review,* May 16, 1959.

4. Buber, Martin. *Between Man and Man.* Tr. by Ronald G. Smith. London: Routledge & Kegan Paul, 1947, pp. 107, 108.

5. Schachtel, Ernest G. *Metamorphosis.* New York: Basic Books, 1959, p. 45.

6. Moustakas, Clark E. *Psychotherapy With Children: The Living Relationship.* New York: Harper Bros., 1959, pp. 17–20.

7. Buber, Martin. *Between Man and Man.* Tr. by Ronald G. Smith. London: Routledge & Kegan Paul, 1947, pp. 112, 113.

8. Moustakas, Clark E. *Loneliness.* Englewood Cliffs, N.J.: Prentice-Hall, 1961, pp. 20–23.

9. Buber, Martin. *Hasidism and Modern Man.* New York: Horizon Press, 1958, pp. 120, 121.

CHAPTER 5

HEALTHY AND NEUROTIC COMPONENTS OF ANGER

I HAVE BECOME INCREASINGLY aware of the way in which anger is used for growth—the way in which its expression releases tensions within a person and paves the way for more honest, deeper ties between persons. I have also become aware of the way in which anger creates barriers and problems, becomes virtually an attack and thus impedes communication and growth. I no longer speak of anger as if it were always one form of human communication. Rather, I view two types of anger: first, a kind of anger rooted in healthy attitudes, aimed at releasing tensions and clarifying and deepening bonds with others, an expression of caring, and the use of one's resources and energies to bring about a fuller, more honest relationship. And, second, a type of anger that grows out of a desire for revenge, out of neurotic roots, aimed at hurting, belittling, and defeating.

I make this distinction because of the recent indiscriminate use of anger in training programs aimed at enhancing self-esteem, promoting assertiveness, and presumably developing stronger individuals. Anger in direct and open terms is often denied and blocked in the growing years, thus leading to unhealthy paths of hostility. To counteract the destructive consequences of repressed anger, encounter groups and other training programs often make open expression of anger an automatic rule of communication. Often, in these situations, no distinction is made between anger that is real, just, fitting, and valid and anger that is unearned, distorted, unfitting, and untrue. No distinction is made between anger that is an expression of the real person and anger that is a form of acting out. There seems to be no recognition of the difference between anger that is releasing and freeing and anger that is misplaced, misdirected, inappropriate.

In my experience with individuals and groups, I have found it necessary to distinguish between *constructive anger*, which ultimately leads to new awarenesses, new bridges of understanding, and respect for differences, and *destructive anger,* which diminishes and punishes. Healthy anger is an immediate response to a situation. It is hot, intense, clear, directed. It reveals and opens paths of communication and, in the flow, enables each person to express what is inside, to disclose feelings of frustration, hurt, and resentment, and ultimately to bring about changes that are consistent with who the person really is. This kind of anger enables each person to put perceptions, thoughts, and feelings out in the open so that each person comes to see the other in a new and different way. Anger, then, is a way to restore something dimming or lost, to bring back and renew values, and to work out differences and animosities that are blocking communication and threatening the relationship. It is a way to bring about necessary changes. Healthy anger relates to basic issues and essential values, not to petty, minor and irrelevant differences. In the process of expressing anger, persons communicate their perceptions and feelings in terms of their own experience, in no way aiming to reduce or defeat the other person. The ultimate goal of anger is to bring feelings clearly into touch with the realities present in each person and to restore a relationship on honest terms. The release of feelings in an unqualified way enables each person more fully to hear, to see, to recognize the other as she or he is.

In contrast, unhealthy anger is a violent act against the other person or persons, a denial of the other's existence, feelings, rights. It is often retaliatory, vengeful, cold, and detached from the relationship. It is a precious ego trip that leaves a chill. Destructive anger is not concerned with consequences and effects. It does not take other persons into account. It is often a one-way message. Since it is not an immediate, spontaneous, and direct outcome of a particular situation, it can easily be scheduled, put into cold storage. In neurotic anger there is no basic awareness of the other or concern for the other, and thus real communication is blocked and distorted. Neurotic anger rather than opening and expanding relations restricts and closes them. It is impervious to the justice and truth of the situation and often takes the form of pronouncements and accusations or indiscriminate acting out. It is often an outgrowth of an elaborate thought process, engagements in fantasy, and a general building up of feelings that are based on assumptions, or fixations, on words, an accumulation of suspicions, and on a great deal of paranoid fantasizing rather than on direct encounter with other persons, on the checking out of assumptions, and on efforts to search into the truth. This type of anger approaches a fetish. The existence of angry feelings in itself is a validation for their expression, without regard to decency, timing, or validity. The presence of anger becomes a sufficient excuse for disrupting, ripping apart, and invading the place where other human beings live.

In therapy, of course, I encourage the expression of neurotic anger. My sole concern is to facilitate its release so that it will no longer sap the person's energies and resources, so that the person will become free to use talents creatively and constructively. I invite the person to punch, kick, mold, slash, use pillows, puppets, punching bags, or other materials to express the raging feelings and release their powerful hold on the person. Within very few limits, the person is free to go all out. The crucial difference is that this occurs through drama and through play. It does not occur in face-to-face attacks that will only diminish relationships when the anger is based on distortions and unrealistic demands.

In therapy, once the anger is fully released, an attempt is made to understand what precipitates the anger. Then the person has the option of making decisions that will not evoke it again and again. The person comes to know that other human beings do not induce anger, rather it is created by the choices one makes and the perceptions and meanings ascribed to others' behaviors. An individual can learn to be responsible, to perceive in new ways and to make changes that do not continually arouse angry scenes with others. An individual can learn to make choices that do not lead to frustrations.

I am not making an appeal to a rational examination of anger, but rather an urgent recognition that anger is legitimate only when it grows out of caring and when it seeks to put relationships on an honest basis. Healthy anger is an immediate response to threat, it stays in the here and now; it keeps the focus on the actual conflict. In no way is the aim to belittle or reduce the other person. The angry confrontation refers to specific issues. Throughout the exchange the basic self of each person is respected and the spirit of what it means to be human while at odds is recognized and affirmed. Thus in healthy anger the human spirit stays alive however intense the expression of feelings and the differences between the persons.

While people working with others in areas of human potentials, communication, and personal growth have contributed significantly to awakening new awarenesses of the destructive consequences of repressed anger, and this has led to increasingly direct expression of feelings that have eventually clarified and deepened relationships, there has not been adequate recognition of the potentially vicious and tyrannical nature of anger. Further more, anger exists in a context—the feelings represent one dimension; the context or focus is also significant. An awareness of the meaning of anger, where it comes from, its significance in the life of the individual person, and its connection with others, are all important components. There are always choices. Is anger the most effective means of settling differences? Though anger often is a powerful expression, it is not always the most healthy way to come to terms with a problem. To make anger an automatic expression in handling conflict is as potentially damaging as automatic repression or appeal to reason. Inner search and struggle are of value, especially when the process enables the person to realize what is distortion or projection and what represents the truth.

Anger is but one form of expression in a hierarchy of choices. Other components may constitute the truth of a moment, the healthier path to take. In other words, what is essential at a particular time in a relationship to maintain the highest level of value? What is essential in communication to keep it alive and full and growing?

As I see it, every significant communication involves feeling, thought, and spirit. I reject outright the assumption that a person can know others fully in an intimate sense only through angry encounters. There are many paths to significant knowing, not simply the sharing of in-depth feelings of anger but also the communicating of essential incidents of the moment and the sharing of crucial transitions of the past and dreams of the future, beliefs and values already formed yet very much alive, immediate challenges, and future opportunity, daring, and risk. There is so much more to the indepth relationship than the communication of feelings. The cognitive and spiritual components, the ideas and ideals a person holds, the situations and projects that inspire, the critical, formative experiences, the parts of the history of moving toward unique selfhood, what inspires and provokes the interests, preferences, and important activities of the person, all go into the making of a significant relationship. The notion that only feelings evoke life or that only anger brings into focus a vivid and exciting world is certainly a limited view and, taken literally, offers an oppressive, tyrannical, and restrictive way. Being alive to all that is present within, and open to what exists in the other, is what constitutes the fundamental in human communication and in interpersonal growth. The communication of these realities, these actual presences—whether related to past, present, or future, and whether primarily thought, feeling or spirit—clearly facilitates the flow of life between persons and deepens the quality of human interaction.

Chapter 6

Honesty, Idiocy, and Manipulation

WHEN I MEET another person fully and completely, I am engaging in an unknown and intangible process. In each of us there is a substance that makes possible a sense of continuity, commitment, and mutuality and enables us to experience a feeling of wholeness and a particular identity.

The striking quality of individual nature appropriates its character through honest self-expression. When I am honest, there is an uncompromising commitment to an authentic existence, to being who I am in any particular moment of experience. No other moment is alive but that moment being lived, and no other existence matters but that which is immediately present. Honesty provides the active moral sense that governs our actions.

I am honest when what I communicate is consistent with my real feelings, even when these depart sharply from the perceptions of others. If twelve people viewing a scene observe that there are eight trees but I see only a pattern of light and color and movement, I claim a configuration, even though all the others see eight trees. The integrating meaning in perception determines the nature of individual reality, not the number of objects or traits tabulated by a machine or observed in a detached manner.

I am speaking of a reality that is decisively different from the objective view, from that of the onlooker and observer who are detached from what they perceive. Buber explains this difference as follows:

> Consequently what they experience in this way, whether it is, as with the observer, a sum of traits, or, as with the onlooker, an existence, neither demands action from them nor inflicts destiny on them. . . . It is a different matter when in a receptive hour of my personal life a man meets me about whom there is something, which I cannot grasp in any objective way at all, that "says something" to me. That does not

mean, says to me what manner of man this is, what is going
on in him, and the like. But it means, says something to me,
addresses something to me, speaks something that enters my
own life (1).

Genuine development of the self requires honesty of expression and a willingness to take a definite position consistent
with what one perceives. Being true to one's own experience is
the central requirement in the continued existence of a real self.
Every distortion of experience creates a false self, pulling the
person in a direction that is less than whole and forcing upon the
self fragments of life; the eyes of another, the heart of another, the
soul of another.

However imperfect one's senses may be, the person alone
feels, touches, hears, and tastes that which is known directly from
experience. Honesty is required; simple, open, direct honesty is
the only way to wholeness, unity, and authenticity of existence.
Honesty is often avoided because it creates conflicts between
one's self and others. In our quest for a truthful existence, we are
often forced to cause suffering and grief to others, and we
ourselves may be deeply hurt in the process. In such moments it is
much easier to avoid the dilemma, to choose the indirect path, to
distort or manipulate the situation, and in some way to avoid facing the truth of a painful experience. The person who persists
retains the integrity of being all there, of remaining in touch with
reality, of continuing to grow as a person, enabling others to know
what is real and be affected by it. The impact of honesty is
described by Gendlin in the following passage:

> . . . I try not to do anything phoney, artificial, untrue,
> distracting or unreal, ever. Of course I do many phoney
> things before I even notice them, but that gives me a chance to
> double back and express the truth. We must help patients live
> with, in and through what *does* confront them, the world they
> *already do* live in. The patient can successfully live only with
> what *is* there. There is no way to live with what is not, with
> falsehoods, with artificial roles played by psychologists. One
> cannot learn to live with the untrue, no matter how good its
> untruth might be. Really, the untrue is not there in a fullness
> that can be lived *with*. On the other hand, saying what is true
> helps because it is already there and one can learn to live with
> it better and differently(2).

The lie gnaws at the center of being, blocks spontaneity, and destroys the integrative quality of the self. The lie is the beginning of a process that leads to self-deception and self-negation. The dynamics involved in this process are quoted by John Shlien from Jean-Paul Sartre's study of schizophrenia:

> The liar, for one thing, is in possession of the truth. He sees both sides. He intends to deceive, and does not hide his intention from himself. . . . It "happens often enough that the liar is more or less the victim of it, that he half persuades himself of it." There's the rub, there's the treachery of it. The lie ("I could not have done that," "It never happened," etc) begun in self-defense slips into self-deception (3).

Being honest in a relationship is at times exceedingly difficult and painful. Yet the moment a person evades the truth, central fibres of the self pull away, and the person initiates a process of deception. Ultimately, deviation from the truth is a form of manipulation, a form of power over the other person or a destructive control of oneself. Evasion, self-denial, and distortion are usually motivated by a wish to influence, change, and direct. Even when fear motivates distortion, the fear is a way of manipulating the other person by preventing the person from discovering real thoughts or feelings.

Conflicts originate between persons when they do not say what they mean and do not do what they say. Dishonesty leads to profound and inevitable destruction. As Martin Buber asserts, " . . . this construes and poisons, again and again and in increasing measure, the situation between myself and the other man, and I, in my internal disintegration, am no longer able to master it but, contrary to all my illusions, have become its slave. By our contradiction, our lie, we foster conflict-situations and give them power over us until they enslave us. From here, there is no way out but by the crucial realization: Everything depends on myself; and the crucial decision: I will straighten myself out" (4).

When I speak of honesty, I do not mean boldly outspoken beliefs stated aggressively and without reserve. Nor do I mean conscious, thought-out, calculated statements intended to provoke and foment, although honesty may sometimes take these forms. I do not mean honesty that is hostile and destructive, which aims to hurt or diminish. I do not mean the aggressive thrust or challenge that aims to attack. I do not mean the "holier-than-thou" attitude that limits and restricts. All of these are other-directed forms of anger that reduce and constrict others and aim at victory and control over others. Honesty, as I know it, means the quiet, direct expressions that sometimes emerge reluctantly, hesitantly, and even fearfully. It refers only to the self of the person, the person's own search for truth, not to the presence or absence of honesty in anyone else. My task in honesty is to maintain an allegiance to my own self, not to hurl catchwords and pet phrases at others. Honesty, as I refer to it, is a struggle for truth within myself, not intended to point out to others their shortcomings and inadequacies or their strengths. What I honestly think or feel reveals who I am. It does not expose or disclose anyone but me.

Even in the presence of the anxiety, pain, and suffering of other persons, I value honesty that is an expression of one's real self; without it reality may be distorted and growth deterred. Honesty enables the person to create an identity, to communicate a real presence, and to establish authentic bonds with others. Being honest is a direct way of introducing one's self, expressing ones ideas, values, and beliefs, and declaring and owning one's feelings. The net effect of continuous, real honesty is the awareness and recognition of one's particularity and individuality. As a result, new potentials are opened and awakened; the person is alive—whether that aliveness takes the form of outward assertiveness or inner serenity. Thus, to be honest is simply to be. Without honesty there is no actual being present; there is no flow of life and no possibility for new life. In its most basic form, honesty has to do with one's own self, one's own feelings, perceptions, and moment-to-moment experiencing. It is the direct communication of the actuality of one's being. In honesty one does not explain or interpret the feelings of others but refers solely to one's own experiencing.

Rarely is honesty the best policy from the standpoint of freedom from suffering or achievement of material gain. In a competitive society, where status, economic prestige, and power are highly prized, the honest person is considered naive, immature, and childlike because his or her chances for success and accomplishment are significantly reduced. Failure of the honest person to achieve respect and happiness is painfully related in Dostoevski's brilliant novel *The Idiot* (5). Myshkin's fate, as an honest and kind man in a society more concerned with wealth, power and conquest than with humanistic ideals, was that of evoking as much distrust as love. Eventually he was defeated and destroyed by a corrupt and dissipated society.

The honest person, trying to live simply, directly, and openly, is often regarded with suspicion and imputed to have evil and hidden motives. Let us examine the way in which some of the characters in *The Idiot* viewed Myshkin. First of all, there was the servant in the Epanchin household who became suspicious when Myshkin answered his questions directly and honestly. Myshkin did not play the role of the visitor, presenting a noble or "class" face, but rather spoke to the servant as an equal, in a way perfectly suitable from man to man but utterly inappropriate from a visitor to a manservant. The servant, overcome with distrust, thought Myshkin was either an imposter or a man soft in the head and devoid of his wits and his dignity. Consider today how much more diverse, complicated, and delineated are the roles undertaken and the games played; how little spontaneity is encouraged and how lengthy the rules and policies governing who speaks to whom, in what way, at what time, and under what conditions. A society that rewards people on the basis of effective role-playing breeds deception and mask-like behavior.

Continuing with the attitudes of distrust and suspicion expressed against Myshkin, Aglaia, who loved him, doubted his veracity, exclaiming, " . . . it's horrid of him to play a part. Is he trying to gain something by it?" Ganya, who was also deeply suspicious of Myshkin, caused him great anguish and treated him as deceitful and devious. In a moving confrontation, bewildered by the fact that Myshkin has completely gained the love and confidence of the Epanchin family in a brief period of time, Ganya attacks Myshkin and calls him a sneak and a liar.

Doubt and suspicion are aroused in the presence of honesty. What lies beneath this man's simplicity? What devious and cunning scheme is being perpetrated? What does he wish to gain? These attitudes were expressed again and again in Myshkin's meetings with others.

Ivan Fyodorovitch remarks to him, "One wouldn't have thought you were that sort of fellow. Why, I looked on you as a philosopher. Ah, the sly dog!" When Myshkin says to Ferdyshtchenko, "I've made you no confession. I simply answered your question." Ferdyshtchenko shouts, "Bravo! Bravo! That's sincere anyway—it's sly and sincere too."

Then there is the analysis of Myshkin's honesty (or idiocy) as an exploitative and selfish condition. Lebedyev's nephew puts it this way: "Yes, prince, one must do you justice, you do know how to make use of your . . . well, illness (to express it politely);

you've managed to offer your friendship and money in such an ingenious way that now it's impossible for an honourable man to take it under any circumstances. That's either a bit too innocent or a bit too clever. . . . You know best which."

Again and again, Myshkin is charged with ulterior motives. Even his most direct, open, and straightforward words are misunderstood and misjudged. He is treated as a curiosity and as a simpleton, with the word "idiot" frequently uttered behind his back. And so to most of us, the honest person is a riddle. What is he or she after? What is in it for them? What is behind the simplicity? What are they trying to get me to do or believe?

A person may speak honestly and sincerely, may answer a question in the light of what actually exists, may speak centrally and at the very heart of the subject, and still not be valued, but rather be belittled and laughed at because what is being expressed is peculiar, unusual, unconventional, or unpopular.

The honest communication can never be understood through explanation and analysis. Efforts to explain, justify, or defend often lead to further alienation in relationships and a sense of hopelessness and despair. Almost inevitably, the motives of the honest person are questioned. The consequence is that the person suffers in a world where the strength and resources of the self are sometimes not enough to maintain a state of health. Myshkin's disintegration, daily reinforced by his awareness of human misery and cruelty, illustrates the inevitable defeat of a truly good and honest man in a morally bankrupt society and is final proof of the inability of any man or woman to bear the burden of moral perfection in an imperfect world.

The honest person wants to communicate in ways that are consistent with actual experiences. It is nonsense to see hidden meanings, unconscious motivations, and thwarted impulses in even simple statements. The honest person experiences conflicts, but they are not rooted in some dreaded past. The basic conflict is one of choice: Whether to be truthful and risk suffering and pain or to maintain a false life and move toward safety and security.

Individuals, living in accordance with the truth of their own experience, face a painful dilemma when they must choose between being kind and being honest, between keeping their word and taking the safe and comfortable way out, between maintaining their integrity and winning the support and approval of others. Though there is danger in pursuing the truth when individuals are at odds with each other, there is also the potential for creating deeper bonds and a more enduring and healthy alliance.

Every dishonest act is a denial of the self. In that moment the person ceases to be. No growth or development takes place; relationships hold stationary. Only by saying what is really believed and felt does the individual participate in reality in a fundamental and healthy sense. Of course, it is essential that honest communication represent something basic, primary, and enduring, not something momentary and fleeting. It is essential that the issues represent something valid, not the results of distortion, misplacement, or projection.

Sometimes it is difficult to speak honestly when the other person is struggling to emerge and is already surrounded by criticism and rejection. Yet I wonder whether being kind and gentle is not always a dodge, an escape from facing the real issue. I wonder if, in actuality, the relationship is not weakened when I act out of kindness though my experience pulls me in another direction. Do I choose to be kind in such moments because honesty is more painful to bear, more uncertain in its effects, more apt to foment unrest and disturbance in a relationship? I have never fully accepted myself when I have been kind at the expense of being honest. As I think through the value involved, I realize that every dishonest act is a denial of the self. Still, I struggle with this issue, and each time I attempt to approach it in a fresh and new way. Ideally, only by saying what I really believe and feel do I participate in reality in a fundamental way.

Often being honest means being different from what one has been before. Suddenly, a new characteristic, idea, or attitude emerges and is viewed with suspicion and disbelief by other persons. We are expected to be consistent, and when we behave differently we are sometimes criticized and rejected.

We are deeply shaken when those we love turn on us in angry tones or suddenly reproach us. Yet many of these situations involve a choice between honesty and kindness. In kindness, we continue to be as we are, meeting others with a consistency of feeling, being supportive and helpful. But the self is always developing in new directions. Sometimes the struggle leads to morbid moods that can create pain and otherwise disturb a relationship in vital ways. Yet if one maintains honesty, living through the misery it sometimes brings, deeper bonds are established and a new beauty and awareness emerge, in the end, which fill life with great joy.

The attitude of honesty in a relationship in psychotherapy is conveyed in an essay by Rebecca M. Osborne. With reference to the severely disturbed individual, she writes:

He senses the shallowness of much of what passes as friendship and the envy and jealousy that lurks in the background of so many family relationships. All of these individuals become part of the conspiracy of *them*. Only the one who can come to the mental patient with genuine acceptance and forebearance in his eyes, saying by his manner as well as his words, "I do not see what you see, but I believe you when you say *you* see it. I believe that you do feel what you claim to feel. Let's talk it over:"—only such a one can win the deep confidence of the mentally ill person (6).

Whether honesty or kindness is chosen when a conflict exists is not a matter of which is better, rather it is the decision of a particular self in a concrete moment of life. Who can say for others whether being and growth are higher values than kindness and the happiness of a gentle laugh? Each person finds the way in a specific moment of life, when theory is totally outside. Then the immediacy of two selves facing each other creates the reality of a joyful experience or one of grief.

The question of honesty first arose in my mind as a serious problem in psychotherapy when I talked with a child about his terrible school existence and the child asked me for an opinion: "Do you believe Mr. Radcliffe, my teacher, should scream at us and hurt us with a ruler when we don't do what he tells us?" And another time when an old man inquired, "Tell me where I went wrong. What did I do to bring so much misery and unhappiness in our lives. Just give me some sign that the evil can be erased, that I can begin to find some decency, some basis for life." Then again with a weary mother whose "mentally-retarded" child had experienced one rejection after another in many schools, a mother who had searched long and exhaustively to find a place where her son could belong. Finally, in defeat, she exclaimed, "There isn't any place for him. No school wants him. No one is willing to help. Why is it that people in the neighborhood avoid and shun him? He is one of our own kind!" And the adolescent who spoke triumphantly and sadistically about the pleasure he derived from throwing a handicapped neighbor down the basement steps, splitting his forehead and necessitating an emergency visit to the hospital—and seven stitches. This youth inquired of me, "Isn't it good for me to feel a victory at last? I've been stepped on and tricked all my life. Now I'm beginning to get even and settle the score. There's nothing wrong with that, is there?"

Each time I held my own feelings in check. Even when my whole being urged a position, urged expression, a part of me held back. I did not speak except to encourage the individual to explore further the nature of his or her own feeling, thinking, and experience. Only later did I realize that in many moments of life clarification and understanding are not enough. Reflections and commentary do not spread to the root of life where the individual lives most deeply. Interpretations too often skirt the edge of existence, stay within the bounds of professional theory and practice, and fail to penetrate to the heart of the matter, which alone will unite two persons struggling to be honest with each other.

Only after much internal dissension did I realize that in many instances to *understand* another person is to place that person on a lower scale of life. It is a kind of leveling process in which a superior insight and intellect grasps its subject and sees into and beyond the surface words and feelings. Yet this seeing into and beyond another places the subject in a category. *He* or *she* is to be understood. *He* or *she* is to change so that I may know my efforts have not been in vain. So that I may measure my success.

I began at times to think, "I want to speak, to say what's in my heart and mind, to meet the other person simply and directly, to come alive with my own expressed conviction." At the same time, I also believed that each person must find the way by the light of individual perceptions, meanings, and values. But the struggle and the search continued until one day I wondered, "Isn't it rather godlike of you to think that your expressed feelings and convictions will influence another human being away from his or her own quantum in life? Aren't you assuming a power over others that in itself implies a view of others as being so fragile and malleable that external ideas will quickly transform them? And doesn't this distort your own experience with individuals, even those who are faced with deep and penetrating conflicts and problems, who in spite of all their suffering have resisted ideas and beliefs that denied their own perceptions and experiences?"

The struggle went on until I realized that the issue could not be settled in advance by theory or assumption or concept or method, but only by life, only by specific transactions between I and Thou.

Honesty is not an old-fashioned virtue, an ideal that has no place in modern life, but rather it is a vital requirement of growth itself, a requirement that perhaps is never completely realized in everyday life. Only as one speaks honestly is there real hope for continued self-identity and for fundamental meeting. As long as one departs from the truth, one continues to remain a stranger to self and others.

Whether honesty is denied for self-protection or for self-aggrandizement, its denial is inevitably a form of manipulation—and manipulation is responsible for much of the human misery, grief, and suffering in the world. I believe that every action, overt or implicit, motivated by a desire to change other persons is a form of manipulation. Although the wish to change others is sometimes couched in altruistic terms, and sometimes even exists as a pure wish for the health and welfare of the other, it still remains as a desire to change and as a form of manipulation, if only by remote control. B. F. Skinner puts it this way: "If, in working with a patient or student or friend, one arranges conditions so that he becomes more active than before and more adaptive, this is progress, but it is also control" (7). I agree that control and manipulation are present if one *arranges* conditions *in order* to change others. But if progress occurs not through arrangement of conditions, not through predetermined goals and criteria for evaluation, but through genuine, spontaneous encounters, then growth occurs naturally. If being one's self has meaning and value for others, if in itself it opens channels of sensitivity, awareness, and discovery in others, then it is like all living substances that awaken in us new dimensions of thought and feeling. I am attempting to make a distinction here between making resources available that may be chosen or not and the calculated use of particular methods and materials in order to change thoughts, feelings, and behavior.

When we are not honest, part of us is buried and a new, false, distorted image replaces the real self. A significant stream of life is removed—a stream that emerged in the first place to meet life, to know persons in the fullest sense, to realize opportunities, to face and resolve the challenges, issues, and problems of existence.

I have come to believe that every form of dishonesty is immoral and is a powerful deterrent to authentic growth. No matter how much I try to deceive myself that by remaining silent I am being noncommittal, when my silence is a form of deception I permit the truth to remain hidden. No matter how much I feel I am following a *professional* ethic when I dodge a question, there are times when I know inwardly a *human* ethic is being violated and I am engaging, through manipulation, in dishonest behavior. No matter how I convince myself that kindness assuages the suffering of others, when it is given at the expense of honesty I know that it is tenuous and false. No matter how much I reassure myself that my desire to change another person is for that person's own good, I know that this wish to change others, even though it leads to "improvement," is an act of manipulation and therefore a form of dishonesty. Even if the person does not resent my desire to change him or her, I am still violating my own belief in autonomy, in the private destiny of each individual, in the responsibility of each self to choose values in living. Even when other persons see my desire to change them as a virtue, the imposition of the views and ideals of one self upon another remains.

When an individual hides behind a screen of objectivity, there is always a danger that the person will successfully control others. Such a protective device makes a true meeting between persons impossible and contributes to the alienation that is so widespread today.

Are we so entrapped in ambition, distortion, and betrayal that we are simply unable to experience the wonder and beauty of life? Is it impossible for people today to relate to sources in the universe that give rise to tenderness and joy? What is it in society that makes it necessary to complicate and obfuscate the simple truths and values of life? How is it that we see the radiant colors of the rainbow and the beautiful sunburst at dawn and yet do not experience grandeur and ecstasy? How do we miss the beauty that surrounds us everywhere?

There is much in the world to pull and tug at me, to arouse within me a sense of optimism, to bring me back to life in all its promise. Then I see the universe as a new creation: The moment of quiet, the silence of rustling leaves, the feel of my footsteps on gathering pine needles, the gentle wind blowing against my face, the soft mist that shrouds the world in a mysterious beauty, the loving message in twinkling eyes, the resonant quality in a compassionate human voice.

Everywhere, all around, we are in the midst of genuine life, yet we reach out and strive for confused and entangled goals, as if the distant star held more meaning and challenge than the immediate and simple truth.

REFERENCES

1. Buber, Martin. *Between Man and Man.* Tr. by Ronald G. Smith. London: Routledge & Kegan Paul, 1947, pp. 8–9.

2. Gendlin, Eugene. "Therapeutic Procedures with Schizophrenic Patients." In *The Theory and Practice of Psychotherapy with Specific Disorders,* ed. by Max Hammer. Springfield, Ill.: Charles C. Thomas, 1972, p. 373.

3. Shlien, John. "The Client-Centered Approach to Schizophrenia: A First Approximation." In *Psychotherapy of the Psychoses,* ed. by Arthur Burton. New York: Basic Books, 1960, p. 297.

4. Buber, Martin. *Hasidism and Modern Man.* New York: Horizon Press, 1958, p. 158.

5. Dostoevski, Feodor. *The Idiot.* New York: Bantam Books, 1958, pp. 52, 135.

6. Osborne, Rebecca M. "The Mental Patient and the Sense of Conspiracy." *Inward Light,* Vol. 33 (Fall, 1960): 26–28.

7. Skinner, B. F. "Cultural Evolution as Viewed by Psychologists." *Daedalus,* Vol. 90 (Summer, 1961): 576.

CHAPTER 7

BEYOND GOOD AND EVIL

W
E KNOW that throughout human history codes of ethics and statutes have been created in the attempt to control human behavior, to point to right and wrong in human affairs. Religious prophets have propounded doctrines that ultimately the good person would be rewarded and the evil one punished. Society has constructed and elaborated notions of what is just and unjust in human affairs and has dictated appropriate contacts among people to protect the individual and to safeguard the welfare of the state. Conformity to social rules is inculcated, both directly and indirectly, at an early age, so that the obedient child is good, while the unruly, deviant child is evil. Social, religious, and legal precepts define good and evil and impose standards on the individual through group pressures and the institutions of society. Good emerges not as a value in its own right, not as a quality intrinsic to being human, but out of a fear of the consequences of being bad, out of a fixed set of laws and standards that presumably protect society from the "evil" individual. Thus, the conformist is good and the rebel is evil, for almost everything that lifts the individual above the herd produces fear and is called evil. The good is not an affirmative expression of a real value, but an act of self-protection and self-preservation. To be good out of fear of the consequences of evil means to choose the system, regardless of one's own self and one's own experience. The good is not something sensed and known through an internal process of awareness, search, and judgment, out of internal articles of faith and belief, but rather what is ordained religiously, socially, and legally to safeguard and protect.

Moral philosophers have not been satisfied with conceptions of good and evil that are rooted in self-protection and self-preservation. They have explored the essence of the good as a quality positively present and necessary for healthy life.

Philosophers have described kinds of goodness and qualities

of goodness. They have employed analogous terms, such as God, love, truth, beauty, justice, harmony, unity, order. For example, Plato in The Republic equates God and good (1). In the Phaedo, Socrates explains that everything that admits of generation is generated from opposites and in no other way (2). Thus, the stronger comes from the weaker, beauty from ugliness, and big from little. Plato contends that anything that has a saving and improving element is good; the corrupting and destroying element is evil. Mildew is the evil of corn, rot of timber, rust of copper. That which is a true part of one's own nature is good; the evil is that which is foreign, contrived, accidental. The four qualities of goodness are courage, temperance, wisdom, and justice; and of evil: injustice, intemperance, cowardice, and ignorance.

Aristotle, in his books on ethics, also describes the qualities of goodness. He explains that the good may be viewed in three different ways: as good in itself, in some quality it has, or in some relation it bears to something else (3). For Aristotle there are degrees of goodness, with happiness having the highest degree of finality—the highest degree of self-sufficiency. We choose happiness for its own sake and for that reason alone, whereas honor, pleasure, wisdom, and other qualities, though good in themselves, are chosen because they contribute to our happiness.

For Epictetus the essence of God is expressed in the essence of the human being. And the essence of the human being is knowledge, intellect, and reason because these attributes distinguish human beings from plants and animals (4).

St. Augustine holds a different view of good and evil. He makes good and being the same: "So long therefore as they are, they are good; therefore whatsoever is, is good" (5). The evil is that which is false, that which is unharmonized and in a state of disorder, that which does not fit or belong. St. Thomas Aquinas takes a similar position: being, the true, the one, and the good are by their very nature one in reality (6).

Hume, on the other hand, sees the good as that which contributes to the peace and security of the individual in society; morality is that which promotes the welfare of society (7). For Hegel the good is a universal which requires individuality to give it life and movement; gifts, capacities, and powers constitute spiritual life, and these are realized only in individuality (8). The good is implicitly inherent in real truth; it is simply being itself.

From this brief philosophical review we can see that different attributes have been selected as virtues: temperance, justice, wisdom, courage, happiness, intelligence, being, harmony, order, reason, knowledge, peace, and security of society. The indicators of evil are: intemperance, injustice, foolishness, misery, ignorance, irrationality disharmony, disorder, war, and disturbance. Each of these qualities describes good or evil in terms of primary characteristics, but none of them answers the question: What is goodness in general? G. E. Moore justifies this failure as follows:

> If I am asked "What is good?" my answer is that good is good, and that is the end of the matter. Or if I am asked, "How is good defined?" my answer is that it cannot be defined, and that is all I have to say about it. But disappointing as these answers may appear, they are of the very last importance. . . . My point is that "good" is a simple notion, just as "yellow" is a simple notion; that, just as you cannot, by any manner of means, explain to anyone who does not already know it, what yellow is, so you cannot explain what good is. . . . The most important sense of "definition" is that in which a definition states what are the parts which invariably compose a certain whole; and in this sense "good" has no definition because it is simple and has no parts (9).

Robert S. Hartman, commenting on the failure of philosophers to provide a definition of goodness in itself, defines the good as that which has all the properties it is supposed to have (10). For example, people are good if they are conscious of themselves and have all the qualities they are supposed to have. The properties of a person attain virtue because that particular person defines them as dimensions of his or her own being.

Martin Buber offers a similar definition. For him the person true to himself or herself is good; the false person is evil (11). There is but one choice: the path of rightness or the path of evil, the path of being or the path of non-being. To be good is to be real, authentic, and true; to be bad is to be fictitious, false, and unauthentic. Truth is an expression of goodness; the lie is an act of evil. For Buber, good and evil are not opposites or extremes of the same reality, rather they are fundamentally dissimilar in nature, structure, and dynamics. The concrete good or the concrete evil is related to specific events and may be recognized during periods of contemplation and self-absorption. The individual knows whether an action is true or false.

Evil concerns itself with possibilities; good is always an immediate and solitary reality. The good is directed—the one stretched beam, the one taut string. For the good, there is only one true path; for the evil person there are many alternatives, many possibilities. The good is a decisive act of the whole self; evil is fraught with indecision and possibility growing out of a detached and fragmented self. Evil needs no confirmation; it reinforces itself as the safe, secure, and wise course. In contrast, the good person requires confirmation.

The ultimate good is the choosing of oneself, even when one's being is not confirmed by others and is independent of all findings. Buber is emphatic on this point:

> The encouragement of his fellowmen does not suffice if self-knowledge demands inner rejection, for self-knowledge is incontestably the more reliable. . . . He must bring the principle of his own self-affirmation, nothing else must remain worthy of affirmation than just that which is affirmed by him; his Yes to himself determines the reason and right of affirmation. If he still concedes any significance to the concept "good" it is this: precisely that which I am (12).

Hartman defines the good in similar terms.

> Thus what I have to do to fulfill my definition (of the good) is to define myself, to answer the question: "Who am I? And Who am I?" I am I. This is my defense of myself—pure self-awareness: I am I. The concept I have to fulfill is "I" or "I am I," and when I fullfill this I am a good "I" (13).

The recognition of the self as a supreme value of life is the birthright of every person. William Saroyan exclaims: "Be grateful for yourself. Yes, for *yourself*. Be thankful. Understand that what a man is is something he *can* be grateful for, and *ought* to be grateful for" (14).

What a person *is* at any particular moment of life may be good, but the individual is born neither with grace nor in sin. In every moment of life every person has a choice—to be and thus to participate in goodness; or not to be, and thus choose to be evil rather than good.

The actualization of a person's capacities and talents toward increasing individuation and uniqueness, toward a particular, incomparable selfhood, is an index of the nature of goodness. But being human also means living in a world of safety, of possibility, of isolation, of embeddedness. Self-preservation is as much a human reality as the sudden, spontaneous, esthetic creation. It is within the nature of the human being to seek and maintain that which is known to provide safety and satisfaction.

If good is desirable and evil is undesirable, if good is a virtue and evil a sin, then the fault lies with human construction itself, for every person in many moments of life is "evil" and every person "good." All good is evil in that it blocks a greater good from emerging. That which has been defined as good can become stagnant, static, and embedded. That which is known as good can become evil and that which is evil can become good.

Evil is good in that it motivates good. Without evil, good could not exist. Good becomes meaningful in contrast to evil; it attains reality by the presence of evil. Together good and evil exist as dimensions of the individual's unity and wholeness.

Perhaps what we must recognize is not the good and the evil in human behavior but the fact that individuals are pressed from all sides to conform. In the light of these constant pressures for conformity, it becomes necessary to encourage and support people in being themselves. A strong and vital stand must be taken in behalf of creative selfhood, not because it is all there is to an individual or because it is all good in contrast to the evil of conformity, but because real individuality is so widely repressed and denied. Left to themselves, individuals will find their own quantum in life; they will choose to be or not to be in the light of the resources and conditions and challenges available to them.

Unfortunately, we are often not able to make a free choice. Doubt and suspicion surround us and pressure us into actions contrary to our own self-knowledge and experience. Because the modern person is pressed to strive for standards, values, and goals that contradict the self, there is continuing danger of becoming a thing, a commodity, a machine. The humanist concern with good encourages creative self-emergence—not mere life, but life with meaning; life with zest; life with self-structure and self-expansion.

The counter influence of the humanist position is necessary to nourish and encourage the expression of true being. Non-being—that is, conformity to external standards and values—is not the more powerful impulse, but it is more strongly encouraged by modern society. The counter revolution is needed to promote the authentic capacities of particular, concrete individuals toward creative selfhood.

Humanism is not good in contrast to the evil of materialism. Both are aspects of what it means to be human. Both are dimensions of the individual self evolving a particular identity while also encountering other selves. The healthy community creates the strong individual; the healthy individual creates a strong community.

REFERENCES

1. Plato. *The Republic*. Tr. by B. Jowett. New York: Vintage Books, 1961, p. 75.

2. Plato. *The Last Days of Socrates*. Tr. by Hugh Tredenick. Baltimore: Penguin Books, 1954, p. 91.

3. Aristotle. *The Ethics of Aristotle*. Tr. by James A. K. Thomason. Baltimore: Penguin Books, 1955, p. 321.

4. Epictetus. *Discourses and Enchiridion*. Tr. by Thomas W. Higginson. New York: Walter J. Black, 1944, pp. 103, 104.

5. St. Augustine. *The Confessions of St. Augustine*. Chicago: Henry Regnery Co.

6. Aquinas, St. Thomas. *Truth*. Chicago: Henry Regnery Co., 1952.

7. Hume, David. *An Inquiry Concerning Human Understanding*. New York: Bobbs-Merrill Co., 1955.

8. Hegel, G. W. F. *The Phenomenology of the Mind*. Tr. by J. B. Baillie. New York: Macmillan Co., 1931.

9. Moore, George E. *Principia Ethica*. Cambridge: Cambridge University Press, 1903, pp. 6–9.

10. Hartman, Robert S. "Individual in Management." Unpublished paper. Columbus, Ohio: Nationwide Management Center, 1963.

11. Buber, Martin. *Good and Evil*. New York: Charles Scribner's Sons, 1952.

12. Buber, Martin. *Good and Evil*. New York: Charles Scribner's Sons, 1952, p. 138.

13. Hartman, Robert S. "Individual in Management." Unpublished paper. Columbus, Ohio: Nationwide Management Center 1963, p. 13.

14. Saroyan, William. *The Human Comedy*. New York: Harcourt Brace and Co., 1943, p. 249.

CHAPTER 8

ETHICAL AND MORAL VALUE

BEING FREE TO BE is the right of every human being. Freedom is necessary to maintain one's humanity; the denial of freedom is equivalent to giving up an essential human characteristic. Freedom without value, however, can lead to destruction and chaos. Freedom within the framework of ethical and moral value means not simply the will to choose but choice growing out of a knowledge of the good and a willingness to choose the good.

A spiritual or esthetic sense is intrinsically present in the ultimate sources of being. To be one's self in the deepest regions means also to be rooted in what is just and true. In Hartman's terms, individuals are good if they have all the properties they are supposed to have as unique persons, including an ethical and moral basis for judgment and action (1).

When *to be* becomes *I am* in actualizing capacities and virtues, then good is present—not only freedom and genuineness but also moral and ethical commitment and responsibility.

When I refer to the good, I do not mean a property or thing that might be labeled as good. Rather, I mean the ultimate moral sense, which is not a law or a definition but the law beyond the law, the internal directive that establishes meaning and value. Morality refers to *value*, not values but the one guiding, determining, necessary light.

A vital relationship exists between moral value and human behavior, between one's philosophy and one's activities, between one's sense of rightness and one's perceptions, feelings, and thoughts. Unfortunately this relationship has not been fully recognized. Too often the concern has been with behavior or with personal and social changes that presumably would result in more effective living.

This does not mean that we should strive to construct final truths which will provide a system of values to be automatically applied. On the contrary, transactions that unite morality and truth are expressed in new and vital ways. Sometimes there is a struggle to find the path, and often that path requires immediate judgment and choices that have not been made before.

By value I do not mean a value system, but rather a basic truth that enhances goodness, touches the individual at the roots of existence, and contributes to a universal good. Although self-choice, freedom of expression, and respect for the individual are important values in the evolution of a healthy personality, they do not permeate character unless they exist in a framework of value or, as Kluckholm says, unless they can be justified morally and esthetically (2). Value refers to worth as an ingredient of being as well as to an ingrained human condition that is infinite and enduring.

A value system refers to beliefs, expectations, and preferences that offer direction and influence choice. But value is an integrating or unifying dimension of the self. It is the quality that renders the person whole in the concrete moments of life. As Dorothy Lee observes, we can speak about human value, but we cannot know it directly (3). We infer value through its expression in behavior.

When we consider value, our inner experience is a feeling of something definite, something absolute, something essential that feels right and belongs. The inner directive (the sense of value) is a commitment to life and to the continuity and enhancement of life in its highest, most ideal forms. The really good is just so, no more, no less (4). This just-so-ness is a unity and wholeness, a harmony of all dimensions of the person.

In modern society, ethical and moral value is not a central force in the development of the individual. In education, the primary focus is on knowledge, skill, and professional competence. In psychotherapy, the concern is with change toward self-confidence, social responsibility, and realness in expression. Family involvement is centered in socialization, enculturation, and adjustment.

But a person may be unusually competent and skillful as a murderer or thief or filled with the kind of confidence that enjoys success and competition by vanquishing others. A free and assertive personality may flourish by manipulating and controlling others, thereby gaining special physical and social benefits. Muscular strength, for example, can be used for battering, defeating, and crushing; or it can be a form of self-discipline. Knowledge can be used for belittling, terrorizing, aggrandizing, or promoting class and caste prejudices; or it can be used in the direction of self-awareness and enlightenment, toward justice, truth, and wisdom. Independence and autonomy can be expressions of exploitation and authoritarian power or they can grow out of a desire to stand out as a real person, to be as one is, to evolve one's unique talents.

It is not enough that the teacher inculcate a thirst for learning, originality, and independence of thought. It is not enough that the therapist facilitate the development of self-direction, spontaneity, and trust. It is not enough that the parent promote personal and social effectiveness. It is not enough for society to condition the individual to a life of comfort, security, group adaptation, and adjustment. It is necessary, as Maslow emphasizes, that education and therapy reach into the moral realm and achieve goodness by helping the individual to become more honest, good, just, beautiful, whole, and integrated (5).

Morality is relevant to healthy existence. Without the ethical and value dimension such gains in personality as release of tension, freedom in self-disclosure, and self-insight are destitute of enduring value. Moral geniuses are not required—but people are needed who are morally alive and able to communicate directly with their fellow beings.

Increasingly, I have become aware that in institutions, such as the church, the family, the school, the clinic, and society in general, we are not concerned in a living, concrete sense with the development of character. Yet it is the moral or ethical base that determines the real meaning of freedom, knowledge, and autonomy. The moral imperative is not the arbitrary ordinance of a transcendent tyrant; nor is it determined by utilitarian calculations or group conventions. The moral law is an individual's own essential nature appearing as commanding authority (6). Such a directive derives meaning in present experience and guides the individual's relationships with others.

Meaning and value are not contained in a quality of mind or attitude but must be determined through actions. Marianne Eckardt warns us that "while the phrase 'to know thyself' has been given much meaning by poets and philosophers, nevertheless, it still leaves us with the clinical experience that self-knowledge is not necessarily identical with more effective or contented living" (7).

The discrepancy that may exist between healthy personality and healthy character was clearly revealed to me when I began to consider my own involvement and that of others in therapy. I have seen individuals change from frightened, withdrawn, guilt-ridden, dependent, repressed persons to open, assertive, real, independent, autonomous beings without evolving in a moral sense.

I remember Don, an adolescent who changed from an inhibited, restricted individual to an outgoing, socially effective person. His parents and teachers regarded the change as a blessing. I, however, became somewhat alarmed when he began to boast about his conquests and achievements over peers with whom he had once felt distinctly inferior.

I was troubled further when he told me triumphantly how his mother would buy a new car with the money she would get from an auto insurance company. By prolonging the recovery of a foot injury, she would receive an increased settlement. Don thought his mother clever and reported excitedly how she had obtained advice from lawyer friends. The goal was to "beat the insurance company at its own game"; strategy, watchful waiting, and feigned indifference on settlement were the key methods. When you had knowledge and influence on your side, you could badger, stall, exploit, and get as much benefit as the situation would allow. I asked Don whether this was honest, whether it was a healthy solution. I questioned him about the meaning of justice in settling the claim, whether fairness and moderation were not more consistent with integrity and rightness. He laughed and said only a fool would fail to exploit the claim to the limits; this was the typical and "normal" way of dealing with insurance companies.

At times, our discussions were extremely heated, with Don expressing anger and disgust at what he considered stupid, naive, and unsophisticated attitudes on my part. Shortly after these confrontations (which unfortunately did not go deep enough or far enough to reach a point of solution), Don's mother terminated the therapy, saying that there was no longer a need for it since Don was now a happy person, achieving in school and successful in his contacts with others. Though the therapy ended "successfully" in terms of the problems that originally brought Don to the clinic, little improvement occurred that influenced his development toward an ethical and moral sense.

Any person concerned with change automatically implies that some or much about behavior is "inferior" or "bad." In education and in therapy (even when teachers and therapists wish to remain dedicated to a theory or to objective procedures), moral and ethical convictions are expressed, even if only subtly and indirectly. Georgene Seward has pointed out that therapists' values are so deeply involved in the process of therapy that they are more than likely to determine the pattern of reconstruction regardless of "honorable intentions" to the contrary (8). Value permeates our development to such a degree that it is never entirely left out of the picture. But it is not a central concern of everyday living or of education and therapy.

I am not suggesting that the educator, psychotherapist, or parent teach value. Direct attempts to teach moral and ethical principles (in contrast to the emergence of value as a dimension of being) are apt to result in failure. Buber describes the pitfalls of a didactic approach.

> I try to explain to my pupils that envy is despicable and at once I feel the secret resistance of those who are poorer than their comrades. I try to explain that it is wicked to bully the weak, and at once I see a suppressed smile on the lips of the strong. I try to explain that lying destroys life and something frightful happens: the worst habitual liar of the class produces a brilliant essay on the destructive power of lying. I have made the fatal mistake of *giving instructions* in ethics, and what I said is accepted as current coin of knowledge; nothing of it is transformed into character building substance (9).

Moral sense cannot be taught or imposed through manipulation and control or through the use of rewards and punishments. Healthy character evolves through confrontations with oneself and others and encounters with life. When I meet another, when I come up against the other person, my sense of value must stand as open and clear, as vital and necessary to my being as a moment of sudden insight or knowledge. I must be present as a whole person and not slip into the role of therapizing or teaching or parenting. I can experience the ethical challenge as an inherent and vital dimension of my world and face this challenge as I might face any human issue or problem.

I am speaking of an organic presence, the importance of holding firm on ethical grounds, staying with the moral sense in the same way that one remains with breathing, as a natural and vital process; in the same way that the tree exists that I meet along the path—simply there, present, full in being. I relate to it as its nature and essence register in me. In this sense, the individual can be present in relations with others, with spiritual, moral, emotional, and intellectual dimensions integrated and unified.

Is success so important to us as therapists, as educators, and as parents that we are willing to avoid the struggle, the pain, the challenge? Are safety and reward so attractive that we remain indifferent in the moral realm because to face the issue, to engage in a battle for moral truth, involves the risk that the gains, changes, or successes will appear meaningless? Do we avoid involvement with another person in the moral realm because at times it is the bitterest battle of all?

In the moral struggle, the therapist is no longer a therapist, and the teacher is no longer a teacher, and the parent is no longer a parent. The whole person becomes involved from the depths of being in a full human struggle of spirit with spirit. The only reality is the emerging battle and search for moral value, which alone gives meaning to life, which alone determines what actually exists between persons in the deepest regions of self to self.

Indifference to value and ethics is a sign of the sickness of man and society. Perhaps this is the most devastating factor of all—the indifference to cruelty and pain; the indifference to brutality and violations of individual and human rights; indifference to the inner voice that a wrong direction is being pursued, that a crime against humanity is being carried out; indifference to everything but one's own status and security; and the expediency of rules and regulations. Indifference in the moral realm grows out of years of indifference to the real self, out of years of conditioning to the system and its routines, procedures, and policies.

The absence of moral value is powerfully illustrated by Yevgeny Yevtushenko in his autobiography. He portrays a scene in which thousands of Russians have crowded into a civic square to see Stalin's coffin and pay him tribute. Suddenly, the mob increases enormously; people are stepped on and crushed. On one side of the square people are blocked by houses, on the other by a row of army trucks. I continue with Yevtushenko's description of the ensuing horror:

> "Get those trucks out of the way!" people howled. "Get them out of here!"
>
> "I can't do it! I have no instructions," a very young, towheaded police officer shouted back from one of the trucks, almost crying with helplessness. And people were being hurtled against the trucks by the crowds, and their heads

smashed. The sides of the trucks were splashed with blood. All at once I felt a savage hatred for everything that had given birth to that "I have no instructions," shouted at a moment when people were dying because of someone's stupidity. For the first time in my life I thought with hatred of the man we were burying. He could not be innocent of the disaster. It was the "no instructions" that had caused the chaos and bloodshed at his funeral. Now I was certain, once and for all, that you must never wait for instructions if human lives are at stake—you must act. I don't know how I did it, but working energetically with my elbows and fists, I found myself thrusting people aside and shouting "Form chains! Form chains! . . ." And now people understood. They joined hands and formed chains. The strong men and I continued to work at it. The whirlpool was slowing down. The crowd was ceasing to be a savage beast. "Women and children into the trucks!" yelled one of the young men. And women and children, passed from hand to hand, sailed over our heads into the trucks (10).

This is entirely the point! We must not live by instructions, by rules, by social, administrative, or therapeutic directives, but by moral strength, individual and universal value, and spiritual strength that is exercised in creating life with other persons, where what really matters is the internal directive that keeps alive the mind and heart and soul of all humanity.

REFERENCES

1. Hartman, Robert S. "Individual in Management." Unpublished paper. Columbus, Ohio: Nationwide Management Center, 1963, p. 13.

2. Kluckhohn, C. "Values and Value Orientations in the Theory of Action: An Exploration in Definition and Classification." In *Toward a General Theory of Action*, ed. by T. Parsons and E. A. Shils. Cambridge: Harvard University Press, 1952.

3. Lee, Dorothy. *Valuing The Self.* Englewood Cliffs, N.J.: Prentice-Hall, 1976, p. 5.

4. Suzuki, Daisetz T. "Human Values in Zen." In *New Knowledge in Human Values*, ed. by A. H. Maslow. New York: Harper Bros., 1959, p. 95.

5. Maslow, A. H. "Notes on Being Psychology." *Journal of Humanistic Psychology*, Vol. 2, No. 2 (Fall, 1962): 59.

6. Tillich, Paul. "Is A Science of Human Values Possible?" In *New Knowledge in Human Values*, ed. by A. H. Maslow. New York: Harper Bros., 1959, p. 195.

7. Eckardt, Marianne H. "Self and Identity: A Magic Deception?" *American Journal of Psychoanalysis*, Vol. 23, No. 1 (1963): 9.

8. Seward, Georgene. "The Relation Between the Psychoanalytic School and Value Problems in Therapy." *American Journal of Psychoanalysis*, Vol. 22, No. 2 (1962): 145.

9. Buber, Martin. *Between Man and Man*. Tr. by Ronald G. Smith. London: Routledge & Kegan Paul, 1947, p. 105.

10. Yevtushenko, Yevgeny. *A Precocious Autobiography*. Tr. by Andrew R. MacAndrew. New York: E. P. Dutton & Co., 1963, pp. 85–86.

CHAPTER 9

SELF-DOUBT AND SELF-INQUIRY

AT CRITICAL POINTS in my life I have seriously questioned the validity of my own existence. Radical challenges and shifts have occurred that have caused me to doubt the reality of my world.

To be alive for me has always meant to be involved with life, to be fully committed to myself and others. From personal involvement and commitment I trusted that life would deepen and that human connections would continue to grow. Without commitment, without relatedness, life would have no meaning. Yet, inevitably, the bonds with others have been threatened by uncertain conditions of living, by shattering experiences, by disease and death, by the search for perfection and morality in an imperfect and immoral world.

The process of human life itself, with its unpredictable and complicated changes, often evokes inconsistent behavior. Contradictions in the self occur; shifts in mood and tempo; changes that cause one to become discouraged and disillusioned. Values that appeared to be enduring suddenly deteriorate. Not only is upheaval inevitable, but love and certainty, moral consistency and integrity are ultimately defeated by the unpredictable breaks in one's pattern of living and by the restless anxiety that is experienced even in a stable existence.

Every person wants to move forward, wants to have new experience and to grow. No relationship remains secure without becoming stagnant and static. As individuals strive for new directions and awakenings, old patterns and bonds are broken, creating a new sense of self—sometimes a feeling of joy, sometimes a feeling of sorrow and despair.

Dissatisfaction with security and repetitive patterns of living is one form of crisis that provokes self-inquiry and self-doubt. This is a central theme in Tolstoi's story *Family Happiness*.

So two months went by and winter came with its cold and snow; and, in spite of his company, I began to feel lonely, that life was repeating itself, that there was nothing new either in him or myself, and that we were merely going back to what had been before. . . . His unbroken calmness provoked me. I loved him as much as ever and was as happy as ever in his love; but my love, instead of increasing, stood still; and another new and disquieting sensation began to creep into my heart. To love him was not enough for me after the happiness I had felt in falling in love. I wanted movement and not a calm course of existence. . . . I suffered most from the feeling that custom was daily petrifying our lives into one fixed shape, that our minds were losing their freedom and becoming enslaved to the steady passionless course of time. The morning always found us cheerful; we were polite at dinner, and affectionate in the evening. . . . I wanted, not what I had got, but a life of struggle; I wanted feeling to be the guide of life, and not life to guide feeling (1).

Existential despair often grows out of the restless inner spirit that seeks variety and excitement. Dostoevski, reacting against the scientific effort of his time, against attempts to calculate how to achieve the good life, describes man's unpredictable and capricious nature, the absolute refusal to be satisfied with happiness and security.

Now I ask you! What can one expect from man since he is a creature endowed with such strange qualities? . . . Give him such economic prosperity that he would have nothing else to do but sleep, eat cakes and busy himself with ensuring the continuation of world history and even then man, out of sheer ingratitude, sheer libel would play you some loathsome trick. . . . It is just his fantastic dreams, his vulgar folly, that he will desire to retain, simply in order to prove to himself (as though that were necessary) that men still are men and not piano keys, which even if played by the laws of nature themselves threaten to be controlled so completely that soon one will be able to desire nothing but by the calendar. . . . I vouch for it, because, after all, the whole work of man seems really to consist in nothing but proving to himself continually that he is a man and not an organ stop (2).

Dissatisfaction with life is motivated not only by a plaguing sense of inertia but also by the complex forces within and without that push toward new paths. During a human crisis, in moments of self-doubt and self-inquiry, questions naturally arise: "Don't you realize no one really belongs? Don't you know nothing lasts; nothing is permanent?" Just at the moment of rest, when the struggle ends, when a strength of identity has emerged, when a relationship reaches a peak of fullness and beauty, just when we truly experience the glory of existence, life is challenged; it is threatened; it is denied.

Through some sudden event, what a person has known and counted on ceases to be. A pattern of life is broken and alienation results. The reality of what is perceived, of all that is valued and loved, is questioned. Important relationships suddenly are experienced in a radically different way. A shattering turbulence calls into doubt the true nature of all life. A search begins to find order and harmony in a universe that now appears to be flighty, unstable, and capricious. Disturbance in the sense of self brought about by a sudden break in a significant relationship is expressed in this poem, written at a time of doubt and disillusionment in my own life.

> I do not know you any more
> Once I felt serene in your presence
> My heart lifted with the joy of lofty ideals
> There was grief and there was laughter
> There was beauty in the love of life and nature
> The budding leaf, the worn oak tree, mud and water on a
>   rainy afternoon, the broken bridge
> The wind on the hilltop, the fragrance of warm bread
>   and cheese, the walk in the sun, and the moon
> Moments of self-fulfillment and love in creation
> Experiences varied and real
> All that existed between us is no more, instead only
>   misty clouds enshroud me
> Manacles to restrict a free heart.
> Is this also an illusion or have I come to face the truth?
> I do not know you any more.

Shattering breaks in what was believed to be an enduring relationship lead to probing self-inquiry: "Who am I? What do I want? Where do I belong? What is truth? What is good? What is real?" How still the beat of the night, how sharply stinging the light of day, the restless roaring of the soul.

I have had many experiences of this kind, in which I entered into my private thoughts in search of meaning and self-knowledge. In such moments, human distance is real and the wilderness grows. Across a barren plain a lonely figure waits for a light which is not an illusion, for a dream which is not a lie. I want to know that the step I take is real, that my heartbeat is my own, that my ideals will not be wasted, that love will not be shattered, that my commitment to life will not be broken, that my dreams will not perish. But how still and silent all is, how barren and meaningless and empty. I hear the mimicry, the mocking voices. I see the critical faces. I go on searching for reality, taking each step with caution, feeling the pain, knowing the horror, experiencing the grief, not giving in but overwhelmed and weakened. I walk for hours, talking to myself, examining my experience, trying to see within, trying to make sense out of the senselessness and shock. As I walk, as I examine the nature of my life, new questions arise: "What does life mean? Where am I going? Does the way I live really matter?" I concentrate on specific experiences that have been important to me, experiences that have been rich, enjoyable, compelling, in an effort to know what is real, what is genuine, what can be counted on in a world of tragic happenings, of unexpected crises, of disease and death.

My search for an enduring life with others continues. I try to find, within my meetings, one consistent, true, perfect, unchanging relationship. But, as I consider my experiences, I see dishonesty, deception, cruelty. New and even frightening facets of the self emerge; new faces and sounds appear, faces and voices I do not know, distorted faces and angry, mocking voices. They may exist but for a moment—yet in that moment they cause me to doubt the reality of my perceptions, the substance of my existence, and to search for an ultimate value in life, for an answer to disturbing experiences with the people I know intimately.

A young student suffering from tuberculosis wrote of the pain she experienced in being abandoned by people she thought were real friends, people who forgot her altogether when her hospitalization became prolonged:

> I wonder if it is not better to have no feelings at all. I know now I have lost my friends, whom I thought to be my friends. Some disappeared when they heard about my illness; others after the first months. There are no more tears to shed; nothing can relieve my pain inside of having lost what seemed

real and loyal and good. It is as if my heart was being squeezed, little by little, and the droplets keep on falling. I think of the beautiful letter my friend once wrote to me. I thought it was really lovely then. Now I know it was only a piece of paper, a friend of the past easily shattered to bits. Why did this illness happen to me? Why? A thousand times I ask but there is no answer.

Another person speaks of the painful disruption in relations he had always felt to be substantial and enduring:

I have had to fight a real bitterness; the one way I have been able to do so is to keep silent, not to speak back in anger or revenge; just take a deep sigh, and go on another day, trying to preserve at least a morsel of inner strength and integrity. I seem to be losing so much; yet this doesn't bother me as I have lost so much already, and my one comfort is within. Many have hurt me, even when they tried to help; many so dear to me, in their advice and friendship, heaped so much hurt, until there isn't anything left to hurt.

No one escapes the pain of ugly and cruel faces and demeaning gestures. Fame and fortune, sickness and death, failure and defeat, strange inner revolutions and upheavals come unexpectedly, unsolicited, unmotivated, unwarranted.

When resources for self-discovery are exhausted, when a person realizes there is no consistent affirmation in life with others, sometimes all that remains is the world of nature. I have watched the movement of clouds on dark, foreboding days until the blackness and the heavy rains engulfed me. I have walked in freezing weather until I felt the unrelenting cold everywhere in my body. On a hot summer day, lying quietly, I have waited for the blazing sun to burn through me. I have felt a relatedness to the harsh rain and the bitter cold and the searing heat. I have felt a completeness in the clouds, in the sun, and in the snow. But, soon the rain ceases; the sun departs; and the freezing cold is gone. And once again I am alone, searching for that person within myself who I can continue to know and be.

At night I have watched the moon until its light radiates through me and, momentarily, I feel I have the answer, but the moon fades away and the light of our communion disappears. I have walked in the early winter woods searching for growing life.

In this silence I find tranquility and beauty. I find peacefulness in being quiet and being alone, but then the blizzard comes and snow covers the forest and my communion with the woods ends.

Once I walked into a damaged neighborhood. Broken glass and paper littered the streets. Everywhere windows were smashed and sounds of decay surrounded me. Yet in this ugliness I stopped to listen to the singing of the birds. I found a shattered bus collapsed in a vacant field. I entered the bus and remained silent for a long, long time, just sitting, sitting and waiting, experiencing tranquility within the ruins, feeling completely comfortable and related to the dilapidated place, listening to the quiet chirping of the birds and feeling suddenly at peace with life. One day in a moment of crisis, I hurried to this place which had become my refuge. Suddenly, I felt a strange stirring, an inner warning that something vital would soon be lost. When I reached the vacant lot, the bus was gone. Once again I stood alone in the ruins, in a broken and wasted land.

Then I remembered one dark afternoon when I watched the crackling embers of a fire. As the light began to fade, I saw images of a life that was being lived by habit, by routine, a life at the call of others, serving, always serving, a life being lived without full awareness of the meaning and significance of existence. Then, suddenly, the inner voice was quelled; the light was darkened; the moment was gone.

Who speaks? Who enters the shadow? What does it all mean? So little real knowing! Only in brief times is the full reality, the full human potential lived, only then is the being within its own soaring spirit, encountering life in all its fleeting, changing patterns. There is no I, no me, no knowing of the self, because in a genuine moment all of life is there, as a whole, in harmony, being lived.

To ask the question is itself a search for a new quiet moment, a search for a new birth, a process of exploring in which there is no answer because turbulence and change are within the matrix of existence itself. Such was the experience of a man who sought a new birth in a new relationship by searching into early experiences in his family. Here, he speaks to me:

> I didn't even know if I loved my mother, I didn't even know if I loved my *own* mother. But everybody loves his own mother. You're supposed to love your own mother. Love her? I didn't even know her. That poor soul lying there in the hospital, staring into space, alive, but seeing nothing, was that

my mother? The doctor said that it was dementia praecox (what is that?) and it wouldn't be good for me to see her. And then when she was getting worse they said maybe if she saw me it would help. And we rode in the car and she didn't say anything and then she looked at me and said that awful "Norman" with its pleading, questioning, worrying, hopeless sound.

And I went back to that private school where I was staying. After class I would go by myself and read the twelve- or thirteen- or God-knows-how-many-volume anthology of the Civil War with its pictures, pictures to stare at. And I stared at them and "Norman," "Norman," "Norman" with that terrible infinite crescendo of a mother's dying dream. But I was only a boy and I couldn't answer, I couldn't answer. I felt the answer inside me but there were no words, only bewilderment. Climb, run, hide, stay where you are. Do something, don't do something, my father, oh, my poor father. And nobody understands and how could I tell my father, tell him what can't be told in words, and these things were always inside me but no words and you just keep them inside and don't know what to do with them. . . . You don't know your mother. Did she ever love you? Vague memories of happy times in the park, vague memories of happy feelings, but when and where. Memories of a bad boy, temper tantrums, hurt mother. Did I cause her illness? Someone once said I did. Did I? Did I? Did I?

And the strange times. She hugged me, desperately, desperately hugged me. Why did you hide those things in the refrigerator? But I didn't, I didn't! She sat there rocking, rocking, rocking. She said I had taken money from her pocketbook and she sat there rocking, rocking. Mother please don't rock like that, please, please. And she rocked and rocked. And she hugged me desperately and we were both bewildered and we reached out in despair into the void between us, futility reached out. . . .

The years went by. Years of numbness and distance. Oh, God, how isolated, how barren is a world in which you can't feel. Time rushes by, with only tiny glimpses into the universe of feeling. It's there but how do you reach it? How? How?"

Yes, in times of doubt and despair the feeling of hopelessness and numbness overwhelms the person. The uncertainty, tentativeness, and provisional nature of human existence are vividly felt.

Again and again the seemingly indelible aspects of the universe slip away. Again and again there is no answer to the question "Who am I?" Self-conscious thought and inquiry are pursued as a way of identifying the self in times of crisis and maintaining individuality in the face of shocking experience. Inner searching and struggling and suffering will always be part of human experience, as reflected in this communication from a friend trying to hang on to a crumbling world:

> Stand alone sometime soon, very soon, before it is too late, before time has run out; stand alone in the dark night and listen and let yourself be spoken to; listen carefully to what the night has to say; listen carefully to the dark colors upon the ground as they cover up and envelop a tree or rock; listen carefully.
>
> And hear, hear that the night is cold; and ask yourself, when will it be warm; and hear, hear what the cold says; it will be warm soon; very soon. But not an inviting warmth; not a sunny warmth; but a violent warmth, a fiery hell, an inferno of terror, and war; war that has already been seething in the darkness.

The person who is consistently confident and sure, who always *knows*, is exhibiting the outcome of routine actions and habits, an attitude grown out of repetition, familiarity, and the status quo. Such a person refuses to see the contradictions that surround her or him and thus denies the inner quest for truth.

None of us wishes to admit that contradictions exist. We count on the familiar, stable, ongoing values; we depend on everyday, intimate relationships. We move in the orbit of those who contribute to our advantage, and we give, in return, out of a sense of loyalty, duty, and love.

Let a severe crisis or calamity come, let there be a shock to existence, and the habits and routines give way. The person is suddenly aware that many aspects of life are far from real, far from genuine, that life has become a standard, uniform pattern. Such an awakening, with its endless questions and competing and opposing wishes and wills, brings with it the realization that in no single relationship can one maintain perfect ethics, pure and consistent humanistic principles. The shattering of a self-image brings with it not only self-doubt and inner disturbance but also doubt of the reality of all life. Such a crisis was faced by Ivan Ilych, the protagonist in Tolstoi's story *The Death of Ivan Ilych*, who thought he had really lived until the day of his sudden, impending death. Ivan struggled painfully with questions of life and death, of truth and reality, of uniformity and individuality, of meaning and absurdity, of grief and unjust suffering. He searched deeply into his life, but no matter how hard he struggled to know he could not understand why he was suffering, why he had to die. He never found the answer, but in his last moments he found a way to live, as revealed in the following passage:

> As soon as the period began which had produced the present Ivan Ilych, all that had then seemed joy now melted before his sight and turned into something trivial and often nasty. . . . His marriage, a mere accident, then the disenchantment that followed it, his wife's bad breath and the sensuality and hypocrisy: then that deadly official life and those preoccupations about money, a year of it, and two, and ten, and twenty, and always the same thing. And the longer it lasted the more deadly it became. "It is as if I had been going downhill while I imagined I was going up. And that is really what it was. I was going up in public opinion, but to the same extent life was ebbing away from me. And now it is all done and there is only death. . . ."
>
> "Yes, it was all not the right thing," he said to himself, "but that's no matter. It can be done. But what is the right thing?" he asked himself, and suddenly grew quiet.
>
> This occurred at the end of the third day, two hours before his death. Just then his schoolboy son had crept softly in and gone up to the bedside. The dying man was still screaming desperately and waving his arms. His hand fell on the boy's head, and the boy caught it, pressed it to his lips, and began to cry.
>
> At that very moment Ivan Ilych fell through and caught sight of the light, and it was revealed to him that though his life had not been what it should have been, this could still be rectified. He asked himself, "What is the right thing?" and grew still, listening. . . .
>
> He sought his former accustomed fear of death and did not find it. Where is it? What death? There was no fear because there was no death.
>
> In place of death there was light (3).

The crisis challenging a dying person is that, regardless of past life, there is an urgent present necessity to discover the real self and to act consistently with the desires, intentions, and will of that self. However falsely the individual may have lived, the search and struggle for meaning continues, if only with the faint stirrings of the soul and the whisperings of a troubled heart and mind.

During critical moments of self-inquiry, I am not I, yet *not* not-I either. I am apart, walking in the sunlight, seeing the broken pieces of life. I enter and hear the whining, complaining voices around me. I speak, but no one listens and no one hears. It is a moment beyond all other moments, and it contains a truth that has not been revealed before. Around me the hurried pace continues, the rugged knock, the impressive face, the shallow embrace. How lucky we all are! The breath I take is a solitary one, heavy amidst the silence of the broken pieces. But I am here. I exist. I am real. There is stillness now, and in that stillness there is a struggle for the dawn, a struggle for a new life of truth, a struggle to accept reality.

Self-inquiry is often a painful process in which life is viewed with a new perspective, a new awareness. What was accepted, as a matter of course, now comes into doubt. Is it real? What does it mean? Was this relationship, this situation, ever genuine? What kind of game have I been playing? The old perceptions no longer hold. Each detail is considered from the vantage point of a self searching for a new identity. At such a time, the person becomes conscious, aware, painfully sensitive. The world will never be the same again. The scenes of life that passed unnoticed before now become sharply real. Their meaning, their value, their genuineness must be considered from the perspective of a new, emerging self. In such moments, I have realized the importance of being absolutely honest with myself. All else becomes secondary. The little remarks, the sidelong glances, the probings and pushings become painful references, and the struggle continues: "Who am I?" "What do I really want?" "What is the meaning of it all?" "Where do I belong?"

But there is no immediate answer, not within myself nor in my relations with others, and not in the universe of nature. Neither love nor comradeship will quiet the anguished self searching for a lasting reality, the painful self in search of authenticity, with all the ranges of the exhaustive peaks and the flat, dark, quiet places. Who asks? Who speaks? Who enters the shadow and the light? There is no final word, only the revolution of a self confronting the reality of life and the apparent absurdity of existence. The process of self-inquiry that follows a human crisis brings with it searing questions: What is life? What is left to mar? Is there no lasting love with love? No answer to the conflict, no indelible way to live? Where am I to be infinitely affirmed? In the stones, in the woods, in the soil? Must life forever be less than whole? Why is it not permanently good and noble, as it was meant to be?

The process of self-doubt initiated by a shock to existence must run its course, must reach its own level before one can live again in the reality of not knowing, in the senseless anxieties of contemporary life, and in the emptiness and meaninglessness of daily habit and routines of work, rest, and play. Then the question of the meaning of life is not asked, not because one knows the answer but because one no longer needs to ask.

There is a return to life, a conviction that love is real, that life has a rich, enduring potential. Even in the darkest hours the individual searches for confirmation of the ideal because the belief persists that human values are enduring. Though the unique life of a person will inevitably be challenged and defeated and crushed, ideals will never be completely eradicated. Though defeat is inevitable, hope and faith are eternal.

The struggle has not been futile. Though there is no permanent answer to the absurdity of existence, the search for meaning leads to real moments of experience. When the inquiry is over, new visions return.

Questions of self-doubt and self-inquiry are not signs of sickness or collapse. The fact that so many persons involved in the struggle to live decently and meaningfully, are asking, "Who am I?" registers emphatically the human response to the existential paradox, to the inevitable conditions of change and upheaval. Viktor Frankl expresses a similar conviction:

> I do not want to give the impression that the existential vacuum in itself represents a mental disease: the doubt whether one's life has a meaning is an existential despair, it is a spiritual distress rather than a mental disease. . . . The search for a meaning to one's existence, even the doubt whether such a meaning can be found at all, is something human and nothing morbid (4).

We all seek consistency. We strive for perfection, for knowledge, for awareness. We all want a permanent union with other human beings, with God, with nature. But there is no absolute consistency; there is no permanency; there is no perfection. Uncertainty, insecurity, temporality, finitude, restlessness, and new awakenings are the ultimate realities of human existence.

No, to ask the question, to inquire into life, to doubt the sensibility of existence, these are not questions of a disturbed and thwarted mind. These are questions that will always be raised, in sickness and in health, because they are rooted in the organic pattern of life itself. And, because we strive for the infinite, we will forever be frustrated and discouraged, forever doomed to suffer. But in the suffering, in the struggle, we find ourselves, our own identity, and a new being is born.

Though the search for permanent answers is bound to be futile, it is a necessary step to creation, to rebirth, to renewal. As individual persons, we return again and again, believing in the fundamental goodness of life. In times of self-doubt and despair all life appears unreal, false, dishonest, even brutal. Then one day you find someone who listens, who loves, someone gentle who feels your presence, and you start gradually to exist again, to feel, to trust, to be a genuine person. You begin to believe in life and to live, without rancor or fear, in the midst of joy and beauty and friendship. The tragedy is over and you have been born anew. Life takes on a sense of permanency. In the midst of this passion for life, there is a continuing sense of self-realizing. Now life is infinite; it is honorable; it is worthwhile. The meaning of life is no longer questioned. The individual experiences not doubt and suspicion but the four great stages of awareness so beautifully illustrated by Van der Post in *The Heart of the Hunter* (5): Life has a meaning only in living, only through creations beyond the immediate self. Acts of creation emerge in the context of a community on earth. Life being lived in a community must be lived as an individual. Individuals must renew themselves by renewing their relationship with God, with the universe, with divine life, beyond the individual and beyond the community.

In the end, out of the broken chain of life circumstances, we choose to live again, however shocking the perfidy is that surrounds us. By choosing to live again we make a commitment to life. This commitment reflects an essential belief and faith in human beings; a conviction that our relation to ourselves, to others, and to the universe is dependable and trustworthy. Transcending the tragedy of the human condition, we recover our belief in our own capacity to live authentically and our belief in the enduring values of faith and love for ourselves, for humanity, and for all that exists in the world and beyond it.

REFERENCES

1. Tolstoi, Leo. "Family Happiness." In *The Death of Ivan Ilych and Other Stories*. New York: New American Library, 1960, pp. 57–58.

2. Dostoevski, Fyodor. *Notes From the Underground and the Grand Inquisitor*. Tr. by Ralph Matlaw. New York: E. P. Dutton & Co., 1960, pp. 27, 28.

3. Tolstoi, Leo. "The Death of Ivan Ilych." In *Quintet*. New York: Medalion Publishing, 1956, pp. 146–156.

4. Frankl, Viktor. "Dynamics, Existence, and Values." *Journal of Existential Psychiatry*, Vol. 2 (Summer, 1961): 12.

5. Van Der Post, Laurens. *The Heart of the Hunter*. New York: William Morrow & Co., 1961, pp. 253–266.

CHAPTER 10

SILENCE AND CREATIVE DISCOVERY

WHEN I SEARCH for the process that encourages, affirms, and supports the growth of individuality, I always arrive at the same conviction—that the primary source of creativity is the individual self. Within the self of each person are potentials for new awareness, for discovery, and for creation of life. These sources of growth are evoked or activated in times of silence, meditation, self-communion, and self-dialogue.

I believe that self-growth begins with an attitude, a receptiveness, a willingness to go wide open, to see what there is, to hear all that is available, to feel and know what is in me and before me. So, I begin by finding a comfortable place, my own special place where I am entirely at home with me. Sometimes I light a candle to recognize this as a special occasion. I sit quietly until I am breathing peacefully, until I am at rest. I let the silence speak to me and I speak to it. I steep myself in this silence to be aware of the wonder of life, the mystery of each new relationship, the joy of creating life with myself and others. I become aware of each meeting as something unique in itself. In this way I am getting ready for the new journey. The silent, meditative life is preparation for communion with others, a way of recognizing each meeting as its own thing, a way of creating a mood that is receptive, welcoming, alive.

My office offers me a place for creative discovery. It is open, the chairs are movable, the floor is carpeted. The person enters and strange and unusual events begin to occur, at once. We are free to move in accordance with the mood and rhythms of our feelings. Sometimes we begin separate and apart. We move closer as the climate of freedom and trust is felt. Sometimes there is an immediate physical contact. The nearness fits and we move immediately into intimate exchange. Life awakens in me during my silence and creates energy and vibrations that immediately enter into my life with others.

Everything is direct, open, spontaneous, immediately available. Nothing is derived, explained, analyzed. The human climate is alive with an immediate invitation to talk, to remain silent, to move; a dance of life—never a secondary process of observing, questioning, directing, interpreting.

My words speak to immediate moments, to root meanings, to felt awarenesses. And my silence is a way of awaiting new life—in absolute quiet, affirmative and supportive, a positive invitation, an inviting glance, a reassuring expression. And thus we begin in a way that encourages and supports individuality and freedom.

In the same way that I create a mood to pave the way to life with others, I create an atmosphere for my own growth when I meditate in silence in a special place that welcomes me; a room that invites me and feels my presence and rejoices in it.

Thus I create an atmosphere of solitude that opens awarenesses and encourages me to talk to myself. These dialogues with myself are essential for me to know who I am being, what I am moving toward, what is basic, and what is unfinished. New perspectives arise, new feelings that awaken me to a clearer recognition of myself, a strong sense of what I am seeking in life.

In times of crisis, I always return to dialogues with myself. It is in this process that I find my openings, that I discover ways for me to be, that I know how to proceed, that I realize what is central in my thinking and feeling. Recently, I sat silently in a hospital setting waiting for what seemed an eternity for my son Steve's surgery to begin. When I found the waiting becoming unbearable, I began writing. The following is what emerged.

The question of being or non-being, of living or dying, is faced at critical moments again and again. Within this struggle is the challenge of remaining alive as a unique and independent self, while at the same time relating with others in an open and authentic way. Recognition of the I (support and encouragement of a particular identity) and the strong response to Thou (in an affirming and unifying sense) are the two central values.

My conviction is that loneliness is a universal phenomenon—the inevitable outcome of the human condition. I believe that rudimentary feelings of loneliness are experienced from the beginning of life and that they reach a peak in awareness during adolescence and again in old age.

In speaking of loneliness, I differentiate between *existential loneliness*, which is a reality of being human, of being aware, and of facing ultimate experiences of upheaval, tragedy, and change, the intrinsic loneliness of being born, of living at the extremes, of dying; and *the anxiety of loneliness,* which is not true loneliness but a defense that attempts to eliminate it by constantly seeking activity with others or by continually keeping busy to avoid facing the crucial questions of life and death. Existential loneliness, with many variations, expresses itself in two basic forms: *the loneliness of solitude,* which is a peaceful state of being alone with the ultimate mystery of life—people, nature, the universe—the harmony and wholeness of existence; and *the loneliness of a broken life,* a life suddenly shattered by betrayal, deceit, rejection, gross misunderstanding, pain, separation, illness, death, tragedy, and crisis that severely alter not only one's sense of self but the world in which one lives, one's relationships, and one's work projects (1).

Feelings of loneliness are especially marked during periods of transition and crisis, and as a response to failures to be and grow in one's self and fulfill one's potentials as a particular individual. Pain and suffering are inevitable during these moments of facing the challenges of living and dying. The search for an answer or a way to continue to live and the agony of conflict and terror severely threaten the sense of self, the meaning of life, and the value of existence itself.

A different kind of loneliness occurs during periods of serenity and well-being. In encounters with nature and universal attractions and in relations with one's own self, loneliness may be experienced as an awakening, as an awareness of beauty, and grandeur, and wonder, and grace. But in moments of crisis and transition, in times of upheaval and rejection, we are confronted with a different choice: The path of alienation or the path of loneliness. My experience in hospitals and clinics, in therapy and in work with families and schools, through letters and published reports, and especially through my own study and search, has revealed, consistently and strikingly, the pain of loneliness and its power in new awareness, self-determination, and movement toward new life.

As I write, I am sitting in a large crowded hospital waiting room while my son, Steve, is undergoing surgery. I am feeling a definite separation from everyone in this room. I am aware within of an anxious anticipation. I look up repeatedly for someone to appear and give me a sign that all is well. As I consider what is happening, I feel a mixture of optimism and hope, a sense that something evil and thwarting is about to end and that Steve will appear with freedom and power and a spontaneous self. I want to be with Steve now in this moment, to feel him through all the locked doors, white costumes, and rituals and medical ceremonies. Everything I have to offer while I wait is for him. So I shut off the sounds, the chattering voices, and all the other noises. There is only Steve and I and the silence that is between us. I wait. My writing eases the tension and focuses my feelings in a way that really matters.

Just now my last moments at Steve's side return. We are moving down the corridor, I freely walking and Steve being pushed on a cart toward the operating room. I breathe deeply to lessen the instant feeling of darkness and pain. Steve has been here in this hospital two long days and until an hour ago he managed to live in his own way, to keep alive his selfhood—wearing jogging clothes instead of pajamas, eating from his suitcase of a half-dozen containers of yogurt and nuts, and occasionally slipping out of the hospital to breathe fresh air, to walk and feel his place in the world. Though we hardly speak in words, there is always a bond between us. He tangibly experiences my support in strange ways. He has been fully alive as a self until now. In the last hours he has been tricked—given a shot of morphine—and now he feels drowsy and very quiet. He wants to walk into surgery, but the orderly insists he must get onto the bed and be rolled in. As we move, tears come into his eyes. Our eyes meet briefly. I struggle to decide what to do. Should I encourage him to speak? Or will I leave these last moments in silence. I try in that last instance to form words, but the tears alone connect us. He is wheeled in for the operation. He has lost control of his destiny. His fate is in unknown hands. I am aware that in the final hour between twilight and blackness he has been robbed of his selfhood. Though this loss is temporary for Steve, the moment is an eternity. I am feeling strongly alone—as I wait I am aware of the impossibility of saying or doing anything that will bridge this gap. I offer my eyes, my heart, one final brief touch. And then he is gone.

I am aware that perhaps, in such a moment, this is all that is required, all that is possible. Yet this human presence in a time of uncertainty makes the difference between the rock-bottom, empty, nothing and the courage to live with loss, to live with fear and loneliness and not sink into it, into the abyss, the depression that is treacherous and eroding of the human spirit, destructive of any hope for real life again.

Isn't this what Frieda Fromm-Reichmann realized when she

lived hour after hour with catatonic patients, staying silently with them, humanly present, waiting for the first sign of life to come, the first movement that would invite her to enter that sealed world, invite her to respond (2)? Perhaps this is what we have to offer any human being who has gone over the brink to the ultimate darkness where there is pain and death at every turn. Only the breath of life itself, the breath of another human being, will restore hope and awaken the desire to live again.

We've come a long way in understanding that loneliness is potentially an opening, a beginning, a process that awakens, encourages, and enables us to experience hope again and to take the first step in active creation of new life.

In the beginning, loneliness is a natural resource for creativity and expression. It's recognition and acceptance lead to strength and courage and new powers of the self. The practice of the lonely journey over and over again exercises essential human qualities and gives the person a resource for renewal and growth. Like any capacity, loneliness must be recognized and nourished and expressed to become a true source of power and life. Suffering is not always defeating and destructive. The suffering in loneliness is an opportunity for creative expression, sometimes through art, music, poetry, meditation, self-dialogue, dance, or other forms of expression.

I wait and wait for Steve to appear. I am becoming increasingly restless and the wait stretches into almost two hours. Finally, I leave the designated room for waiting and stand just outside the operating room. Everything appears more vivid—the bright, glistening snow outside the window, the gloomy, grey, sterile hallway. At last a cart is moved out of the operating room and Steve is being wheeled back to his room. He speaks one word of recognition but it is enough for now. For in that word is a definiteness that tells me that he is once more in charge of his life, that now he is a free man.

Silence is at the heart of this process, a respect for that silence, a willingness to let it be, to let it grow in its own form and move in its own direction. I know now I must be patient with my silence. It has something to offer me, and I must let it emerge into what it is to be. I know I will not remain in darkness forever. My waiting, of course, must be patient and accepting and caring if the silence is to grow into something fresh, vital, and newly born. There are silences that are corrosive, obtrusive, poisonous, ugly— the nervous silence, the demanding silence, the tense silence, the condemning silence, the sarcastic silence, the belittling silence. All of these diminish, restrict, deny the right of silence to exist, to be, to create. These are all forms of silence gone sour, signs of failure to respect silence as a source of new energy and creation.

Life flows when silence is welcomed, when what is just opening or beginning to be is supported and permitted to expand, when what one is offering oneself in silence is affirmed with patience. It is in this patient silence that new bonds with oneself are established. Again and again in my work and life with others, my silent presence is singled out as a key in the emergence of awareness, determination, and new action. It is a form of absolute belief that something of value exists long before there is any direct evidence to support that belief.

Ronald Fox put forth, in strong terms, his conviction that silence really is golden (3). He states that there are points in one's growth when communicating with others is actually detrimental to further development. He discovered that when he shared his plan to write a novel and discussed his ideas with others, he was no longer able to write—even though he was listened to and supported. He believed he had made a fundamental mistake and concluded: "There is a point at which I can either write or I can talk about it but at which I cannot do both. I know this is true. I knew it in my head and I know it in my heart. It is the truth for me. It has always been the truth with me, but I have not always known that I knew it."

From his own experience and from his experiences with others in therapy, Fox altered his approach, deciding that there were times when he would serve his "patients better by asking that they not share some ventures with him, that they remain silent about them, and that they go ahead and do them."

Sam Keen has proposed a way in which silent dialogue in connection with negative emotions serves the person toward new awareness:

> There is a moment in the downward spiral of any "negative" emotion (fear, anxiety, despair) when an escape route opens up. Stop running away from the dreaded thing. Turn slowly. Face it. Walk deeper into the anxiety and know the pain. Cease resisting (evil?). Breathe deeply. Soften your body and mind and let the full force of the rejected feeling into your awareness. Listen. Be attentive to the voice of the pain. Invite it to speak to you about your life. What is it trying

to tell you? "Negative" emotions are much like repressed and dispossessed peoples in the body-politic. They cease to be destructive when they are invited into full participation in the commonwealth. Repress them and there will be insurrection rather than resurrection (4).

And Rich Blair describes his valuing of solitude and imagination in silence:

> For some time I have been intoxicated with the wholly unexpected nature of new images which absorb me in moments of solitude. Often, I retreat to a particular chair I like, snuggle in until I'm comfortable, and wait for the echoes of my day's activities to recede. All at once, a calm and unity swells up from within me, reverberating and vast, and I feel at the threshold of a new frontier of Being. Each breath intakes and enlargens the immensity of this threshold, my extremities tingle with excitement, and a new image emerges as a sudden event without presentiment or thought. This image, a new image whispering its own impassioned reality, often unprecedented in my experience, not causally connected with the past, is a simple image sufficient onto itself. I believe this whisper to be the voice of my spirit, and this image to be the poetry of my spirit. A new image, a new world!
>
> While I occasionally search for meaning in antecedent experiences from my past which may contribute to the onset of an image, more often I am concerned with the essential newness and freshness of the image. I wish to listen to, feel, smell and taste this ripening fruit of my spirit, and allow a new meaning to emerge and surprise me, I wish only to be receptive. . . (5).

I hope by now that you the reader are in a quiet mood. I would like to invite you to locate your source of silence in an activity of meditation and solitude.

Find a place in a room that is just the right spot for you, where you are comfortable, almost weightless, as the unique individual you are. Shake all the parts of your body so that you feel loose and unrestrained. Sway from side to side and become comfortable. Find a sense of unity, a center within yourself.

Now I don't have to tell you the value of being able to do this in everyday life. Most people are pulled off center during some time each day. Roshi adds: "And some are pulled off of it more or less every hour of the day. I have gone into shops and offices and the like and seen people just as I've talked to them almost go splat on the sidewalk or on the floor of the office they are working in, simply because they have not learned to be at peace within the center of themselves; and you're not going to learn that until you stop the racket inside your own head and stop being annoyed by external things."

Nobody can get inside you and make you be still. You have to learn the degree of alertness it takes not to be hijacked by your own thoughts and emotions.

Be at peace within the center of yourself. Thoughts or feelings will come through. Just let them pass.

What you have to do is remain still, as if you were beneath a bridge. Overhead the traffic is passing. It is of no concern of yours. Although you know it is there, you just remain peaceful. If you get caught up in sounds and smells or movements, don't feel you have ruined your meditation. Just note that you have been hijacked and come back.

You meditate in order to become completely you, as you are for you. Be at peace within the center of yourself (6).

Let your breathing become quiet and rhythmical, until you feel completely at rest. Imagine yourself to be a bubble on the bottom of a glass of water. As the bubble rises to the top be aware of a thought or feeling within you. End the thought or feeling when the bubble reaches the top. Again become a bubble at the bottom of the glass and form a new thought or feeling. Each time begin with "I think" or "I feel." Continue with this process until you have exhausted all thoughts and feelings that are within you at this time, until you feel completely satisfied and relaxed (7).

Now let us end this meditative session with an experience of free movement. Select a piece of music that inspires and awakens in you a sense of absolute joy. Remove whatever clothing would be impeding or restraining. Remember in this you must be fully committed, deeply involved, and willing to let go in unrestrained, unstructured movements. As Kazantzakis exclaims: "We bless the Lord by dancing. Because dancing kills the ego and once the ego has been killed, there is no further obstacle to prevent you from joining with God." All is dancing and nothing else. So move with everything that is in you, with everything that you are meant to be.

Some may say that all I have offered you are images, that I

have only awakened desires and memories, that these are only reflections on one theme, like photographs to remind and awaken an awareness of life's potentials. Perhaps that is what I offer in an effort to evoke and expand consciousness. If so, let these expressions remain photographically vivid for now and always and let them inspire dreams and a determination to find a new self, to create a new life.

REFERENCES

1. Moustakas, Clark. *Loneliness and Love.* Englewood Cliffs, N.J.: Prentice-Hall, 1972, p. 20.

2. Fromm-Reichmann, Frieda. "Loneliness." *Psychiatry* 22 (1959): 1–16.

3. Fox, Ronald. "What If Silence Is Really Golden?" *Journal of Contemporary Psychotherapy* 6 (1974): 165–167.

4. Keen, Sam. *Beginnings Without End.* New York: Harper & Row, 1975, p. 9.

5. Blair, Richard. Solitude and Imagination. Unpublished essay. Detroit, Michigan: The Merrill-Palmer Institute, 1976.

6. Roshi, Jiyu Kenneth. "On Meditation." *Journal of Transpersonal Psychology* 6 (1974): 111–123.

7. LeShan, Lawrence. *How To Meditate.* Boston: Little, Brown & Co., 1974, pp. 82, 83.

CHAPTER 11

DIMENSIONS OF THE CREATIVE LIFE

EVERY HUMAN BEING has the potential for living creatively, for relating authentically with others while maintaining a distinctive and unique individuality. In spite of this inherent capacity, we have often turned away from ourselves and each other. We have moved toward a life of material gain, surface communication, and safe, conventional relationships. Most meetings are conforming interactions between ghosts of people rather than exciting, fundamental human exchanges. Most meetings are based on intellectual habits and external guides, on the values of the system or, as Ken Kesey calls it, "the combine" rather than on the values of the self (1).

When people are genuinely related, they create for themselves and each other new feelings, new experiences, and a new life They learn to trust the mystery and wonder in themselves and in the world and thus journey into an expanding awareness and an enlarging reality. But when a person says something that is appraised and adjusted, reacted to and balanced off, when a person speaks in order to put ideas in "proper perspective" and to compete for status, then the person is no longer present as an integrated being. The person is reacting, participating as a reactor to external events, to the outside of people, and to things. There is no spontaneity or involvement, no real living. Talking is the object of talk, and the flow of words suppresses the anxiety that should be felt from meaningless and empty conversation.

Unfortunately, modern society does not encourage diversity and individuality, does not center on genuine interhuman experiences between real persons. Ambitious parents set up goals and communicate expectations indirectly and deviously, so that what they really want and expect from the child registers clearly at subliminal levels regardless of what they actually say. Or, quite openly, parents program the child's life so he or she progresses step by step toward parental values, goals, and expectations.

Often the individual is unaware that the unique growing self has been cancelled out and in its place is only a definition of what should be—and that that definition is so pieced together that the individual lacks substance and identity. The living qualities of individuality and self-awareness remain hidden, dwarfed, and undeveloped.

The self is not its concept any more than a tree (or any living thing) is its definition. The parts of an individual pieced together do not make an integrated whole. They are fragments of a self blocked from achievement of unity through denial of real feelings, real desires, real interests, and self values. Presumably, to be average is the safe goal. But regardless of theories of numbers and mechanics, the average is merely a statistical construct. It is not the healthy path. For all its safety and comfort, the golden mean is still only a fictitious and mechanical number. It exists in fantasy, although that fantasy may be more real for "average" persons than reality itself.

Unfortunately, the "average" does not remain in tables and charts and textbooks; it finds its way into schools and into the dead process of modern education. The activities in modern schools are often mechanical and unimaginative, and the already alienated child is grouped and lesson-planned so that he or she takes one more step into exile and moves farther and farther away from a unique selfhood. At last the child becomes convinced that he or she is average and that averageness is all there is. The child rejects the one dimension that can still bring meaning to existence—his or her own yes-feeling. The values and resources that exist within the deep regions of the self have not been tapped and explored, and so the individual becomes one of the sea of faces, one of the modulated and patterned voices. Along with the subject matter, the individual becomes programmed.

The child became that way in the first place because he or she was not valued and confirmed as a self. Parents did not take their cues from the child, did not love the child as an independent self with strange and peculiar avenues of expression. They did not help the child to open up new territories that would derive their initial value from the self, from the movements of the body, from a growing awareness of life, and from a wish to explore life on its own terms.

The child learns to take cues from the outside, learns to do what is proper, what is approved. Motivated by the right incentives, by the right rewards, the child adjusts to external circumstances, plays the game, and carries out the appropriate role. In the process, the unique heritage of the child as a particular person is obliterated. Adjustment becomes the goal of life, and rewards come in the form of materialistic and social benefits. But, at the same time, individuals are reduced to collective modes, to the least common denominator, to a mechanical way of life. Lacking ethical and moral commitment, denying the realization of higher ideals, repressing the imaginative, daring, and creative ventures that characterize the spontaneous life of unique persons, the individual becomes more an object or thing than a real person with real feelings, real interests, and real talents.

Motivation is often used to trap attention and coerce effort, to persuade people to engage in projects that have no intrinsic worth. Tensions are developed within the individual that must then be resolved through achievement and activity. Strivings for equilibrium, release of tensions, and death wishes are erroneous representations of human life. The tendency to seek and maintain an existent, or "safe," state is characteristic of sick people—a sign of anomaly and decay (2). In the healthy person, autonomy, spontaneity, and self-direction are the guiding forces in a creative life. Motivating a person to adjust is an external means of influencing that leads to inauthentic, conformist living. Adjustment is not a positive assertion of the self. It does not indicate who a person is and what the person stands for; it is a form of giving in to external pressures.

The alienated individual experiences a constant vague sense of anxiety. Life is brief, time passes, and the authentic sources of being are drying up. More and more the limit of time becomes a threatening realization, and a sense of incompleteness and despair often overwhelms the person. This is the despair of self-abrogation and self-denial.

Three methods or attitudes of modern living contribute to the deterioration of uniqueness and individuality and the development of mass behavior and mass identity: *analysis, diagnosis,* and *evaluation.* By such approaches we seek and find the weaknesses and inadequacies, the abnormalities and deviations in ourselves and others. We set up norms, establish categories, and create hierarchies that close the doors of perception and predispose individuals to look for and find in themselves and in the world the objects and fragments of "good" living rather than the good life itself. We create classes, castes, and divisions that separate individuals from their own spontaneous inclinations, resources, and values. We create categorical distinctions and competitive strivings for victory and glory. We become judgmental and place standards on other people's strivings and creations. Sometimes we think that through diagnosis, analysis, and evaluation we can find the hidden pieces of a puzzle and put them together to form an insightful picture, but such a scheme is effective only in a closed system. Humanity is not bounded by fences and frames. At any moment the person can cast the picture puzzle to the winds and make a choice that alters the entire nature of existence.

We can never find our real selves or any other person through diagnosis, evaluation, or analysis. These methods break up the self, objectify it, and make finite what is essentially personal, unified, and infinite. They are inevitably fixed in the past and fail to recognize the emerging powers of choice and promise, and the sudden new awarenesses, discoveries, and creations of a unique growing person. Inevitably, analysis is a destructive approach, looking as it does behind reality for causes and events instead of recognizing that reality is contained in the immediate experiences of the person and in an unfolding life. Progoff affirms this position in the following statement:

> When the person becomes self-consciously analytical, the momentum of growth is lost. This is so for several reasons, any one of which can permanently stunt the process of creative development. One reason is that when the person begins to think of himself in the light of pathology his image grows dim. The thoughts he projects are thoughts of weakness and they refer to the difficulties experienced along the road of development rather than to the unfolding essence of the process as a whole. When they are described and diagnosed and are given the respectability of pathologic forms, they become entities with a reality of their own. The focus of attention is then placed upon the transient pathology of the process and the energy latent in the seed of potentiality is not drawn upon (3).

Analytical knowledge, despite all its content of "truth," remains fragmentary and limited. A life based on this kind of knowledge does not flow from the spontaneous creative powers of the self but from external signs and directions. Persons with severe emotional problems do not need diagnosis and analysis. What is required is genuine human experience, meetings with real persons. Then the capacity for living and experiencing may still be able to evoke creative life.

A science that objectifies, evaluates, and puts people in categories eliminates the real persons. It sets up impersonal and unalterable standards and categories based on fragmented views of behavior. It deals with elements of sameness. Such a science abstracts until, eventually, persons and things become nothing at all. For example, a flower is nothing when we analyze it and abstract its characteristics and qualities, but it is positively a flower when we enjoy it in absorption with nature. The reality of experience and the personal creations of the individual can never be known in analysis and abstraction, can never be known by precise measurement, but only through immediate, unified experience. The unique and idiosyncratic qualities of experience cannot be observed, defined, and classified but must *be lived to be really known.* John Steinbeck and Edward F. Ricketts express this view in the following passage:

> We knew that what we would see and record and construct would be warped, as all knowledge patterns are warped, first, by the collective pressure and stream of our time and race, second by the thrust of our individual personalities. But knowing this, we might not fall into too many holes—we might maintain some balance between our warp and the separate thing, the external reality. The oneness of these two might take its contribution from both. For example: the Mexican sierra has "XVII-15-IX" spines in the dorsal fin. These can easily be counted. But if the fish sounds and nearly escapes and finally comes in over the rail, his colors pulsing and his tail beating the air, a whole new relational externality has come into being—an entity which is more than the sum of the fish plus the fisherman. The only way to count the spines of the sierra unaffected by this second relational reality is to sit in a laboratory, open an evil-smelling jar, remove a stiff colorless fish from formalin solution, count the spines, and write the truth "D.XVII-15-IX". There you have recorded a reality which cannot be assailed, probably the least important reality concerning either the fish or yourself.
>
> It is good to know what you are doing. The man with his pickled fish has set down one truth and has recorded in his experience many lies. The fish is not that color, that texture, that dead, nor does he smell that way (4).

The creative life always involves a concern with life as a whole. It is always based on self values, not on the values of the system.

Creative living involves meetings between real persons in which each expresses himself or herself, not within a prescribed role, not as an expert, not in accordance with rules and conventions, but as a person with unified skills and talents, a person who lives wholly within the requirements of each situation. The result of such experience may be the emergence of an enlightened and open person or the return to health of an emotionally sick one. But such change is the natural outcome of important human experiences. It is not something to be sought for, but something that happens.

INTRINSIC NATURE, BEING, AND BECOMING

Three central, orienting concepts of self are: *intrinsic nature, being,* and *becoming* (5). Intrinsic nature refers to the natural, inherent, given, unchanging potentialities or proclivities of a person. The challenge is to develop these potentials as fully and completely as possible. Inner nature is universally non-comparable, absolute, inviolate. Its focus, orientation, and unity in any one individual is always unique.

There is no such thing as *a type* of person (except for "useful" abstracting purposes). The experience of one's separateness as a human being represents both the necessity and the opportunity for the person to manifest basic tendencies, to develop a personality. The continuing creation of uniqueness is guided by values, based upon the unconscious or pre-conscious perceptions of our own nature, of our own "call" in life.

The harmony and emergence of one's own life seem to come from the increasing capacity to find in the world that which also obtains within the depths of one's own being. The self emerges in appropriate patterns of experience that incorporate the inherent truth of the unique person. Being refers to this concrete, holistic patterning of self in immediate living, as well as the unyielding, absolute, and unique qualities of the individual person. The individual self, or being, is an ultimate core of reality which remains unchanged throughout changes of its qualities or states. To be, a person must be true to himself or herself. The sources for the assertion of human potentialities are deep within the personal experiences of the one who asserts them. And one can discover the real self only as an autonomous entity. Being is good as itself and can be understood as a whole only in itself alone—not in terms of its attributes. It is an indivisible unity.

True experience is the natural expression of one's inner self in interaction with people and resources. As such, all expressions in true experience are creative. True experience involves an immanent orientation characterized by the immediate knowing of the world through direct, personal perception. All the significant undertakings of our past lives are embedded in our present selves and cannot be isolated without violating the essence of experience.

The individual is engaged in life in the present, with a forward thrust in the future. This is the concept of becoming, with its implications of change and transformation. Creation is conceived as a continual transition from one form to another. The world, while it is being perceived, is being created by an individual who is a process, not a product. The individual is not a fixed entity, but a center of experience involving the creative synthesis of relations. The central force for this becoming nature of the person is a basic striving to assert and expand one's self-determination, to create one's own fate.

Every person has unique and unusual potentialities. And because the person possesses these capacities, there is an inherent thrust to realize them. The fulfillment of these needs represents the self-actualization of the individual and the constant emerging of self, of one's "nature" in the world. Failure to actualize essential capacities is equivalent to non-being.

Consistent with his or her intrinsic nature, the individual develops certain appropriate needs, sensitivities, inhibitions, and moral values—both in love and in friction, but always in accordance with the real self. To the extent that painful experiences foster and fulfill our inner nature, they are desirable experiences. Growth in self-fulfilling persons comes through struggle, agony, and conflict, as well as through tranquility, joy, and love.

UNITY AND SELF-CONSISTENCY

Personal growth as portrayed here stresses the unity and organization of the unique individual. Personality is conceived of as an organization of values that are consistent with one another. In all personal transformations, certain persistent and distinguish-able characteristics and values remain.

In a real sense there is a whole: the totality of being. To view the person in parts is not only invalid but a denial of the integrity and respect entitled to every human being, a denial of the person's right to be regarded as a whole person. Segmented behavior is an expression of the individual's effort to remove a condition that interferes with unity and self-actualization.

The real person responds entirely and wholly, organizing and unifying perceptions of the immediate personal world so that they have appropriate value and meaning. The life of the individual is an organized, patterned process, a distinctiveness of pattern that constitutes both the unity and distinctiveness of self. All past processes obtain their specific function from the unifying overall pattern of the individual. The necessity to maintain this unity of the self is a universal, dynamic principle.

How do persons know they are growing in terms of their unique potentials, according to their own special human resources? There is no objective way of knowing, no external evidence by which this question can be answered. Only through subjective, inner experiences and convictions in moments of solitude does one come to feel the authenticity of being. A letter written by the poet Rilke in response to a young writer who sought his advice beautifully expresses the importance of inner searching.

> You ask whether your verses are good. You ask me. You have asked others before. You send them to magazines. You compare them with other poems, and you are disturbed when certain editors reject your efforts. Now (since you have allowed me to advise you) I beg you to give up all that. . . . A work of art is good if it has sprung from necessity. In this nature of its origin lies the judgment of it: there is no other. Therefore, my dear sir, I know no advice for you save this: go into yourself and test the deeps in which your life takes rise; at its source you will find the answer to the question whether you must create. Accept it, just as it sounds without inquiring into it. Perhaps it will turn out that you are called to be an artist. Then take that destiny upon yourself and bear it, its burden and its greatness, without ever asking what recompense might come from outside. For the creator must be a world for himself and find everything in himself and in Nature to whom he has attached himself . . . (6).

The truly human relationship is an encounter in which two persons meet simply and openly in a spirit of unity. In such a relationship nothing intervenes—no system of ideas, no foreknowledge, no aims. It is a matter of full person-to-person presence rather than of individuals acting and being acted upon.

Sometimes it is necessary for one person to help another gain the courage and strength to act on his or her own. A famous passage from Plato's *Seventh Letter* emphasizes this point: "After much converse about the matter itself and a life lived together, suddenly a light as it were, is kindled in one soul by a flame that leaps to it from another, and thereafter sustains itself. . . ."

It is truly a matter of touching something within a person, bringing into activity a potential already present but temporarily blocked or stifled. It means freeing other persons to recover their own nature, to express themselves, and to discover their capacities. Every act of helping others to fulfill their potentials is at the same time an actualization of one's own capacity for meeting persons as persons and valuing them as they are.

In the creative relationship, changes occur not because one person deliberately sets out to influence and alter the behavior or attitude of another person, but because it is inevitable that when individuals really meet as persons and live together in a fundamental sense they will modify their behavior so that it is consistent with values and ideals that lead to self-realizing and communal ends. The creative relationship is an experience of mutual involvement, commitment, and participation—a meeting of real persons. It can be studied or "learned" in a static and discrete sense, but it can only be known through living.

The life of any person or thing is its own. All that another person can do to aid the development of that person is to affect the environment in which potentialities can be fulfilled. Materials and resources can be provided that may enrich experience, but in real growth the individual alone determines the direction. Tenderness, care, personal warmth, and confirmation all affect the development of the individual and the enhancement of the self.

It is within the power of every person to treasure personality; to strengthen and value individuality; to turn toward honesty, affection, and self-respect, toward intellectual and aesthetic growth; and to turn away from destructive analysis, self-degradation, alienation, hypocrisy, cruelty, cowardliness, and smallness.

In the creative human relationship there is a feeling that soars beyond the limits of self-awareness and into the heart of another person. There is a feeling of oneness, a feeling of communion. There is the freedom of being that enables each person to be spontaneous and responsible. Freedom means opening oneself to the positive potentials and uniqueness of a relationship. It means allowing whatever will happen to happen, not forcing the direction or the results, but expressing talents and skills immediately, spontaneously, and in accordance with the unique requirements of each human situation.

REFERENCES

1. Kesey, Ken. *One Flew Over the Cuckoo's Nest.* New York: Viking Press, 1962.
2. Goldstein, Kurt. *The Organism.* New York: American Book Co., 1939.
3. Progoff, Ira. *The Symbolic and The Real.* New York: Julian Press, 1963, p. 60.
4. Steinbeck, John, and Ricketts, Edward F. *Sea of Cortez.* New York: Viking Press, 1941, p. 2.
5. Moustakas, Clark, ed. *The Self: Explorations in Personal Growth.* New York: Harper & Row, 1956, pp. 271–273.
6. Rilke, Rainer Maria. *Letters to a Young Poet,* 2nd ed., rev. Tr. by M. D. Herter Norton. New York: W. W. Norton & Co., 1954, pp. 17–22.